SPLASH

SPLASH
Show People Love And Share Him

Ken & Paula Hemphill

Travelers Rest, South Carolina
www.auxanopress.com

First Print: December 2007, Second Print: March 2008
Third Print: November 2008

Project Manager: Kenneth W. Priest; Creative Design/Layout: Christi Butler;
Creative Audio/Video: Gordon Butler; Editing: Helen E. Spore

Copyright © 2007 by Ken Hemphill
All rights reserved.
Printed in the United States of America

ISBN-13: 978-1500288419

Published by Auxano Press,
Travelers Rest, South Carolina
www.auxanopress.com

Scripture quotations taken from the New American Standard Bible®,
Copyright © 1960, 1962, 1963, 1968, 1971, 1972, 1973, 1975, 1977, 1995
by The Lockman Foundation. Used by permission.
www.Lockman.org

*To those who endeavor to splash
living water on all they meet.*

PREFACE

It was bath time for Lois, our first granddaughter. She was only six months old, and the kitchen sink became a viable substitute for a baby bath. Did I mention that Lois is a beautiful, blue-eyed blonde who can move every muscle in her body at the same moment? It was apparent that Lois enjoyed the warm water and the attention of all the adults who had to assist in the bathing of one tiny infant.

As the bath progressed, she became increasingly animated. Arms began to move with enthusiasm as if she were directing an unseen orchestra. Soon, the legs joined the symphony of unheard music as she became even more comfortable with her surroundings. It was only a matter of minutes before all of those participating in bathing Lois were nearly as wet as she was. I have since had the joy of joining in the festivities of bathing Lois and her slightly younger cousin, Emerson. In virtually every instance, I have been thoroughly *splashed* by their exuberance.

As I ponder those bath time experiences, I am convicted that sharing one's faith ought to be more like my granddaughters' sharing their bath with all those who dare come within range of joyous splashing. Christians should *splash* everyone they meet with the Living Water of the Gospel. **SPLASH** represents a simple acrostic—*Show People Love And Share Him.* When I read the New Testament and look at the life and ministry of Jesus, I notice that there is nothing strained or artificial about His witnessing. It is natural, spontaneous, and joyous.

The very mention of splashing water reminds us of Jesus' encounter with the woman at the well. He splashes a little water on her the moment He speaks with her in a public place. He has her attention, and that is all it takes for her to begin to get soaked with the Gospel. When Jesus asks the woman to draw water for Him, the saturation process is well under way. Even when He confronts her with the reality of her sinful life, she is impressed that she has met a man who knows all about her and yet still loves her. She has been *splashed.* Jesus shows her love and shares the truth of who He is.

Those who measure such things indicate that only about 4% of those who claim to have a personal relationship with Christ have ever told anyone about that relationship. Why? I think most Christians want their friends to know the joy of a personal relationship with Christ and to have the assurance of an eternal home in heaven. Yet for most of us, witnessing seems a bit forced and artificial. We have made it a program to grow the church, and only a small number of "brave individuals" sign up for "evangelism training." Witnessing is not only about growing the church. It is about sharing the greatest news ever conceived with our friends, neighbors, colleagues, and, yes, even our enemies.

In our well-meaning attempt to train people to witness, we may have made witnessing—which should be simple, natural, and spontaneous—into something that is complex, unnatural, and often canned. We have implied that "the witness" must attend weeks of training, memorize a list of Bible verses, and be prepared to answer every objection a skeptic might throw his/her way before he/she is ready to brave the waters of personal evangelism.

This is not another program!

What you have in your hand is not another evangelism program. This is the "un-program." Sharing the story of one's personal relationship with Christ should be both natural and fun. If believers are truly experiencing an abundant relationship with Christ, then those who cross our paths on a daily basis should be getting splashed by Living Water. So, this book is designed to assist you in developing a more intimate relationship with Christ.

You have probably guessed by this point that the word *Splash* is a focal point of the little book you have in your hand. You are most perceptive. The acrostic **SPLASH** stands for *Show People Love And Share Him*. Witnessing is nothing more than telling your own story in the power of the Holy Spirit. This book is

ix

designed to give you both the confidence and practical suggestions that enable you to splash Living Water on everyone you meet.

I believe the most natural setting for splashing people with the Gospel is where you live, work, and play. This study is designed to help you find natural and supernatural ways to build relationships. This will enable you to share the greatest news ever heard on planet earth—man can have a personal relationship with his Creator, know his sins have been forgiven, and have an eternal home in heaven when he dies. Who wouldn't want to hear that news?

How to proceed with the study.

As you look through this book, you will find it is actually a Bible study about the life and ministry of Jesus, the Master evangelist. I believe that you will find the study both interesting and challenging. Each week, as you study one aspect of the life and ministry of Jesus, you will be asked to consider ways to adapt the principles learned from the ministry of Jesus to your own personal lifestyle.

The reading assignments are both brief and biblical. Since the chapters are short, I would encourage you to take the time to read the referenced Bible stories in their entirety. The Holy Spirit will use the Word to inform and transform you. At the end of each section, you will be asked to respond to a few simple questions about the biblical narratives. Ask the Holy Spirit to teach you and take the time to write answers in this workbook in the spaces provided for you. If you do this study in the context of a small group, working through the questions at home will prepare you to participate more fully in group discussion. You can, of course, do the study on your own, but the greatest impact will come as you discuss and pray about the ideas presented in this material with like-minded believers.

The study will work in any context. Your family could be your small group or you might want to consider inviting a few believers from your neighborhood to join you for the study. Church groups also might choose to use the study in Sunday school, cell groups, discipleship groups, etc. You decide how the material can best be used in your setting.

A brief overview.

During the first week, you will discover how Jesus *Showed* the Gospel. Jesus combined demonstration with verbalization. This one-two punch gave tremendous impact to His ministry. I have some good news. To *Show* the Gospel you don't have to be perfect. You simply have to be in love with Jesus and be filled with the Spirit. Be real and be yourself! Then Jesus will *Show* through you.

The second week will build naturally on the first as you focus on the ministry of Jesus to *People*. Jesus saw people's needs and their potential. We often miss the very people God places in our path because we see faceless crowds instead of unique individuals. You will be invited to look at persons who are already in your Splash Zone.

People respond naturally and spontaneously to *Love*. People from all walks of life were drawn to Jesus because they sensed His love for them. Enjoy thinking about simple ways to show people love. By the way, this love does not depend on you; it is the work of the Holy Spirit.

And does not sound like a very impressive word, but I think you will find this to be one of your favorite chapters. Many believers think they have done enough when they show people love, but the truth is most people won't link your loving action to your relationship with the Creator of the universe if you don't tell them. We will study together how Jesus linked the verbal gospel to the visible gospel.

The word *Share* indicates that evangelism involves sharing oneself. Jesus was willing to touch the leper, speak to an outcast woman, and go to the home of Zacchaeus. He shared Himself with others. Evangelism is not about giving some "canned" speech or presentation. It is not dependent on our ability to answer all the difficult questions of life. When we share our lives with others, we find it creates receptivity for the Gospel.

The word *Him* tells us that the Gospel is Jesus. Jesus kept pointing people to Himself as the Living Water, the Bread of Life, and the only way to the Father. Most people have not rejected a relationship with Christ; they have rejected religion. You have wonderful good news. Sinful man can have a personal relationship with a Holy God because of the provision He has made through the gift of His Son.

You may think it is important for believers to be involved in the life of the church if they are to grow in Christ and you may perceive that *SPLASH* doesn't seem to focus on the church. That would be a wrong assumption. Once people develop a personal relationship with Jesus—the Head of the Church, you will find that they desire and need a place of worship and service in the church. Your friends will be receptive to your conversations about your church once they are "born again." Newborn believers have an insatiable appetite for the pure milk of the Word (1 Peter 2:2). As their brother/sister in Christ, you can and must tell them about the family of faith that provides such nourishment for you. They will then be responsive to this message since the Holy Spirit now indwells them.

I pray that this study will begin a wonderful new chapter in your life. You will see opportunities every day to Splash your family, friends, neighbors, and colleagues with the good news of Christ. You will discover that *Splashing* becomes a natural part of your life that is supernaturally empowered. For additional information about the *SPLASH* process, see our web site: www.splashinfo.com.

GLOSSARY

Splash Zone This is your sphere of influence.

SEP Splash Effectiveness Partner

SHOW

A friend of mine who pastors a Nazarene church told me about an interesting conversation he had with a young man he had recently led to Christ. He was impressed that this new convert not only showed up for church on Sunday but also that he was faithful to come on Wednesday evening for Bible Study. He was intrigued by this development for two reasons. First, many of his "more mature" members did not consistently attend on Wednesday night and second, this gentleman made his living mowing yards. That meant summer was his prime time to generate his income and thus his normal six-day schedule was from 7:30 A.M. to 7:30 P.M. The pastor knew that he was giving up several hours of daylight to come to church on Wednesday night.

Thinking he might learn something that would help him build Wednesday night attendance, the pastor decided to ask the new believer why he left work early to attend Bible study. He not only learned something about how to improve attendance, he learned more than he ever expected.

Making Wednesday Bible Study a priority required the landscaper to have all his employees stop working by 4:30 and bring their equipment back to the shop. He did this for two reasons—he needed that mid-week spiritual boost, but he also wanted his employees to see that something was different about him. In other words, this new believer knew that this radical act of shutting down early would "show" his employees that he was a changed man. His desire for God's Word and God's people outweighed his desire to make a little extra money.

It may sound simple but it has provided a profound way for this man to "show" his story so that one day he may "share Him."

The community was buzzing with excitement. Simon, a prominent Pharisee had plucked up the courage to invite Jesus to his home for dinner. He had also invited several of his best friends. We all believed that he was afraid to be seen alone with Jesus.

Inquiring minds wanted to know—was he interested in becoming a follower of this radical teacher from Galilee? Was he simply curious about the man who had healing power? Who could blame him for wanting to meet Jesus? Everybody had been talking about Jesus since he had raised the widow's son near the town called Nain. We were all wondering if there would be theological fireworks during the meal. Animosity was already growing between the popular teacher and the religious establishment. Most of us believed that Simon was setting a trap with the goal of finding some reason to accuse Jesus of heretical teaching.

In truth, it is difficult to recall exactly what we thought might happen. Opinions throughout the community varied, but none of us in our wildest imaginations had conjured up an event as unexpected as the one that actually occurred.

A woman with a questionable reputation in town decided to crash the dinner party. Somehow, she found her way undetected to the feet of Jesus, but her presence was soon exposed as the pungent aroma of fragrant oil filled the room. To the absolute horror of the host, this sinful woman began to weep, literally washing Jesus' feet with her tears. To top it off, she took down her long hair, an act unheard of among respectable Jewish women, and began wiping the feet of Jesus. She was so overwhelmed that she alternated between kissing, drying, and anointing.

You can imagine the reaction of the Pharisee. He was incensed that a sinful woman had entered his home, but he was even more surprised that a man regarded by many to be a prophet had allowed this sinner to touch him. He told Jesus in no uncertain terms of his disappointment, announcing to those at table with him, "If this man were a prophet He would know who and what sort of person this woman is who is touching Him, that she is a sinner." (Luke 7:39).

Jesus, however, was unshaken by the awkwardness of the moment and the stinging rebuke. He actually used the events of the evening to teach an unforgettable lesson. First, he asked Simon a simple question about a creditor who forgave two debtors, one owing ten times more than the other. He asked, "So which of them will love him more?" (Luke 7:42b). Simon was forced to respond that the one who had been forgiven most would certainly be most responsive.

Jesus now put the woman center stage as he reminded Simon that as host he had ignored even the common courtesies of water to wash the feet or a kiss of greeting while the woman had wet his feet with tears and even showered them with kisses. The contrast between Simon and the sinful woman could not have been more apparent. What Jesus did next is still being talked about on the streets today. He looked at the sinful woman and declared, "Your sins have been forgiven." (Luke 7:48). Everyone was shocked by the presumption of the rabbi. "Who is this man who even forgives sins?" (7:49).

You'll never believe what happened next. Jesus ignored the angry protests of the dinner party guests and focused His attention on the woman. He gently declared, "Your faith has saved you; go in peace" (Luke 7:50).

Who is this man from Galilee? The whole community is talking about the dinner party. We have been touched by His tenderness for a sinful woman. His courage and kindness have set the streets ablaze with conversation. "I must meet him for myself!"

Perhaps you recognized my fictional retelling of the story taken from the seventh chapter of Luke. We could have chosen virtually any story from the life of Jesus to make our point. Speaking to the woman at the well, touching an unclean leper, telling a guilty adulteress that He did not condemn her, or inviting Himself to the home of Zacchaeus—all are actions that show the love of God. Jesus practiced grace in the flesh. He not only shared the good news, He embodied it.

If we are going to be effective in sharing the good news in the marketplace of our everyday existence, if we are going to splash our friends and colleagues with the Living Water, we must first show people love. We must *illustrate* the Gospel in order to earn the right to *articulate* the Gospel. In this first chapter we will look at the life of Jesus for clues to help us learn how to show people love.

A Few Foundational Principles

Let's lay a little groundwork before we begin our study. There are a few principles that must be understood and agreed upon before we move ahead.

God is everywhere and is always at work advancing His kingdom. Let me take a burden off your shoulders from the very beginning. It is not up to you to "win someone to Christ." The convincing and winning are the work of the Spirit. It is the work of God through the Holy Spirit to convict persons of sin and draw them to Christ. God, however, does use human instruments as He advances His kingdom on earth. Thus, kingdom persons constantly ask the Father to show them where He is at work, and then they join His activity. Let me illustrate this from the life of Jesus.

In John 5, we find the story of Jesus healing the man by the pool of Bethesda. Jesus instructed the man to take up his bedroll and walk. Don't forget that this event occurred on the Sabbath, which means it was illegal for the man to pick up the bedroll. So, Jesus had not only broken the Sabbath requirements Himself, but he had also caused the "formerly" lame man to do the same.

5

The Jews began persecuting Jesus for His flagrant disregard for the Sabbath. Jesus response was simple but stunning. "My Father is working until now, and I Myself am working" (John 5:17). Here's my paraphrase: "You don't like my healing this man on the Sabbath? Take it up with my Dad. When I saw my Father at work healing the man, I simply asked if I could have the privilege of being the instrument He used to bring His healing."

Now, the Jews were upset over two things—Jesus' disregard for the Sabbath and the audacity exhibited in calling God His own Father. It is at this point that Jesus explained two concepts which we must clearly understand and adopt if we are to be effective in reaching those in our splash zone. First, He declared that the Son is not capable of doing anything on His own (5:19). If the Son was fully dependent on the Father to show people love, then we must also admit our own total dependence. Showing God's love is not something we are capable of accomplishing on our own, nor is it something we are called to do in our own power. It is the work of the Spirit who desires to bear fruit through our lives.

Second, Jesus indicated that He only participated in activities which He saw His Father doing. In other words, He simply looked for the activity of the Father and joined with Him in that work (5:19). You might be wondering how Jesus learned to see the activity of the Father? The answer may surprise you: "For the Father loves the Son, and shows Him all things that He Himself is doing" (John 5:20a). The Son, who in His incarnation was fully man, simply asked the Father to reveal what He was doing.

This verse radically changed my prayer life. I knew that I was a son of God through my new birth, and I knew that the Father loved me. I was left to ask why I didn't see His activity in my world today. Have you ever wondered the same thing? I realized I had never asked the Father to show me what He was doing. When the Spirit revealed this truth to me, I began asking the Father to make me aware of His kingdom activity as it occurred.

This simple prayer totally transformed my perspective. As the Father answered my prayer, I discovered that once I began to see His activity in real time, it became increasingly easier to recognize it. You have probably been around a hunter or a birdwatcher who has developed an uncanny skill of seeing an animal or bird when no one else notices its presence. Likewise, when you ask the Father to show you His kingdom activity, you will find that He joyfully gives you the ability to see Him at work and to join Him in that work.

Have you ever asked the Father to show you what He is doing? Take the challenge and watch what happens as the Father shows you His activity. Why not pause and do that right now? He will empower you to see people from His perspective.

Prayer is the key to seeing God at work and showing people love. We touched on this point above, but it is so critical that we must underline it once more. Our natural tendency is to think that we can actually do something for God in our own strength. We know we must rely on Him when it comes to the really difficult stuff, but we ignore our constant need. We must agree with the Son that we can do nothing apart from God's power. "Nothing" means nothing! It is in our admission of our absolute and ultimate dependency that we discover the key to praying without ceasing. Prayer is an all-day, ongoing dialogue with our Father. Just talk with Him like an ever-present friend. Ask Him to show you His activity, to give you the boldness to join Him, and to *Show* you how to demonstrate love.

You can't see God's activity and you can't show God's love without the empowering of the Holy Spirit. It is the Spirit who enables you to see God at work, and it is the Spirit who produces the fruit of God's character through you, thus enabling you to *show* people love. As you study this material, ask God to quicken your mind.

The harvest is abundant. One of the barriers we face is our fear that people are resistant to the Gospel. That is simply not true! The Gospel is by definition "good news." Everybody likes to hear "good news." When you find a good restaurant or happen upon a good sale at a local store, you love to share that news with someone you care about. They, in turn, are delighted to hear that good news. Our news is the best news possible—God desires to enter into a personal relationship with man, and He has made that possible through the gift of His own Son.

The problem is, we have not often shown that what we have to share is "good news." Most people have not rejected the "good news;" they have rejected religion. We are called to share a relationship, not a religion. People are interested in relationships and most have never thought that they are worthy of entering into a relationship with Holy God. You have good news that people need to hear and want to hear.

In case you are still skeptical about the abundance of the harvest, let me refer you to the expert in this field. Here's what Jesus said—"The harvest is plentiful, but the laborers are few; therefore beseech the Lord of the harvest to send out laborers into His harvest" (Luke 10:2). Can we take Jesus at His word? Yes! We can, and we must! The issue is not with the harvest. The reason we are reaching so few people is that we have refused to go into the field and gather the harvest that has already been promised. Notice once again that Jesus indicates the key to sending out workers is prayer.

Being a witness is not an option. I often hear believers talk about witnessing as if it is an optional part of the Christian life—like adding a six disk changer to the order form for your new car. A witness is what we are before it is what we do! It is what we experience before it is what we declare! Once you have encountered the Living Lord, you are a witness of His saving grace.

Luke ends his gospel with the account of Jesus' appearance to His disciples. Two of the disciples meet Jesus on the road to Emmaus. When Jesus eats with them, breaking the bread and blessing it, their eyes are opened, and they recognize Him as the risen Lord.

They return to Jerusalem to find the Eleven and describe to them what occurred on the road to Emmaus. As they are telling their story, Jesus stands among the gathered disciples. He shows them His hands and feet, offering them the opportunity to touch Him and see that He is truly alive. After He instructs them from the Scriptures, He makes a simple declaration—"You are witnesses of these things. (Luke 24:48). They were there; they had seen and heard Him, and thus, they were forever witnesses of these things. Their presence and their experience made them witnesses. Their effectiveness in sharing their witness would depend upon the Spirit and not their own insight. Thus, they were instructed to wait until they were empowered from on high.

Let's think about it this way. If you were to see an accident or a crime occur, you would be a witness to that event. You might argue that you really don't want to be a witness since it may require you to give a testimony. Guess what—that is really not an option. A lawyer will likely subpoena you, and you will be required to give your account of the event. You are a witness! Your presence and your experience make you one.

In our case, we are witnesses to the greatest good news ever conceived—the sovereign God of the universe desires to enter into a love relationship with sinful man, and He paid the price to make it possible. Our experience of His grace and the presence of His Spirit in our lives make us a witness.

Perhaps you are thinking that you can't memorize a list of verses or overcome your fear of talking to a friend about spiritual matters. Don't worry; you don't have to memorize anything, and you don't have to pluck up your courage. The Holy Spirit will give you the recall and the courage to tell your story.

Get the Salt out of the Shaker

In his inaugural kingdom message, Jesus declared, "You are the salt of the earth; but if the salt has become tasteless, how can it be made salty again? It is no longer good for anything, except to be thrown out and trampled under foot by men" (Matthew 5:13). Once again, we need to notice the declaration is "we are salt." Being "salt" is no more an option than being a witness. If we belong to the King, we are, by virtue of that relationship, the salt of the earth.

To be salt has numerous implications. First, before the advent of refrigeration, salt was used to preserve food. Thus, our lives should be such that they have a preserving effect on others. Simply put, we stop the rot! Our lifestyle—our presence, our language, and our behavior—should have a preserving influence.

How do you respond when you are around those whose language has a putrefying effect? What should you do when people at the office begin to say things that destroy the reputation of a colleague? What would be the proper reaction to racist or filthy jokes? What do you say when someone uses the Lord's name in vain? How would salt respond to such rot? These moments, when properly seized, can be a forum to show the Gospel.

We can't respond with a "holier than thou attitude," but we can shake a little salt out of the shaker. Lovingly tell the person that you prefer not to listen to jokes or stories that belittle persons created in the image of God. When they use the Lord's name in vain, just respond that you would rather they not talk about your Father in such a harsh manner. The person may ask you what you mean, and you can splash a little Living Water on them.

Second, all of us know that salt brings out the flavor of food. In fact, sometimes health conditions mandate that persons maintain a salt-free diet. This is called a "bland diet" and for good reason. Food without appropriate seasoning has little flavor. The Christian should add flavor to life. Our zest for living life stems from our relationship with the Creator and from the understanding that He desires for us to experience abundant life (John 10:10). The sheer joy with which the Christian approaches life will show people Christ.

Our ability to express hope and even joy in the midst of adverse circumstances arises from our confidence that God is at work in everything for our good (Romans 8:28). Such personal and biblical convictions show the people around us the power of the Gospel. Every event and encounter of our daily experience provides a platform for us to show the Gospel. All we must do is get the salt out of the shaker.

My wife recently went through cancer surgery and chemotherapy. Her response to these challenges was used by the Holy Spirit to flavor life for many. She was honest about her fears and failures as well as her joys and triumphs. Her transparency and confidence showed the power of the Gospel at work in her life. The cancer and her response to this difficult situation provided a visible platform for showing the power of God to work in every circumstance for our good. What are you dealing with right now that might actually be a platform to show the love of Jesus to others?

Third, salt also makes you thirsty. I love popcorn, but I can't eat popcorn without craving something to drink. Our lives should be such that they make those around us thirsty for Jesus. As we read the gospels, we are constantly impressed by the eagerness of those who sought out Jesus. Why? Because they discovered that He was salt. He made life flavorful. He put people's needs over rigorous attention to the legalism surrounding the Sabbath. He accepted people for who they were but loved them too much to allow them to remain the same. He called for and expected the best of people.

Our lives in Christ are designed to make people thirsty for the Gospel. Your conviction of God's power will enable you to live with zest, thus making others curious about the hope within you. The purity and joy of your lifestyle should cause others to desire the Christ who lives in you. Don't be anxious about not being up to the task. This is the work of the Spirit as He produces fruit in your life. Get the salt out! *Show People Love And Share Him*!

Hallowed Be Thy Name

In response to a disciple's request that Jesus teach them how to pray, Jesus first indicates that they should begin with the simple declaration—"Father, hallowed be Your name" (Luke 11:2). Why is this the first statement of the disciples' prayer, and what does it mean? Does it simply mean that we give God our permission for His name to be holy? Of course not; God's name is holy because God is holy. When the Jews encountered God's memorial name, YHWH, in Scripture, they inserted the title Adonai in its place because of the holiness of God's name. What, then, does it mean to say, "Hallowed be Thy Name?"

It means that we are asking God to hallow His name in our lives, to reveal His character through us. We refer to John 17 as the great High Priestly prayer of Jesus. In the first thoughts of that prayer, Jesus speaks of glorifying the Father on earth by completing the work that the Father gave Him to do. He then declares, "I have manifested Your name to the men whom You gave Me out of the world" (17:6). In other words, the work of Jesus was to reveal the Father's name or the Father's character.

This concept is so important that the Son's last promise to His Father before the passion and crucifixion was this: "I made Your name known to them and will make it known, so the love You have loved Me with may be in them and I may be in them" (17:26). The future tense verb "will make" must relate to the events that will soon transpire—the mock trial, flogging, and crucifixion. The singular desire of the Son is that these events will provide the platform for Him to make the Father's name known. Jesus' response to His persecutors will have an evangelistic impact—the Father's love will be demonstrated to them.

Do you daily pray that the Father will "hallow" His name through your life? If not, why not start now? You will be amazed at how such a simple prayer will create a radical attitude adjustment. Before I respond in anger to someone who mistreats me, I must ask myself, "Will my behavior reveal my Father's character? Will it help me share the good news or keep me from it?"

Have you ever heard someone argue that the hypocrites are keeping them from becoming a Christian? I think that is a pretty weak excuse, and yet, I am afraid that we have given many potential believers the excuse they are looking for. Is there any evidence that the Father lives in you? Are you growing in your family resemblance? Remember, we must show Him if we are to be effective in sharing Him.

Learn from the Master

One of my favorite stories in Scripture is the encounter of Jesus and the Samaritan woman by the well (John 4). Virtually every element of this story shows the Gospel.

Some of the Jews who had been scattered by the Babylonian captivity had intermarried with Gentiles, creating a people called Samaritans. Samaritans were considered half-breeds. They had created a place of worship separate from the Jews. This particular Samaritan woman had several strikes against her. One big strike was she had been married five times and was currently living with a man who was not her husband. Her presence at the well late in the day indicates that she is not welcome at the well when respectable women are present. She is even looked down upon by the Samaritans.

Jesus distinguishes Himself from the norm when He speaks to this outcast woman. He actually asks her to do Him the favor of giving Him a drink. She is startled that a Jew would ask a Samaritan woman for a drink. This demonstration of the Gospel opens a venue for the declaration. Then Jesus is able to tell her of water that would quench one's thirst for eternity.

While Jesus does not ignore the reality of the woman's sin, He refocuses the conversation by insisting that true worship is an issue of one's spiritual condition. The woman does not feel condemned in the presence of Jesus, but rather she knows she is encountering One who has splashed her with Living Water. Many of the Samaritans from that town believe because of her testimony. She had met a man who tells her everything she ever did. The implication is that Jesus pointed to her sin to bring liberation and not condemnation.

Another familiar story is found in John 8. The scribes and Pharisees caught a woman in the very act of adultery. They proudly parade the woman into the temple complex to the center of a group of persons listening to Jesus teach. It is apparent that those who demand stoning are not concerned for the woman or the Law of Moses. Instead, they are interested in trapping Jesus into ignoring the letter of the law or ignoring the plight of the woman. The woman is nothing more than a tool for their own agenda.

Every eye was on Jesus as He stooped to write on the ground. The accusers persistently demanded that

Jesus pronounce judgment upon the woman who is the center of attention. Jesus declared that the person without sin should cast the first stone. In the awkward silence, He stooped to write once again. When Jesus stood, no one remained but Jesus and the woman. Jesus compassionately told her He did not condemn her but that she must not return to her sin. Once again, Jesus demonstrated grace. If it is true that a picture is worth a thousand words, then this message of forgiveness was one those gathered in the Temple that day would never forget.

"Zacchaeus was a wee little man; a wee little man was he." Thus go the words of a little childhood ditty that I loved to sing. Today, we might say that Zacchaeus was vertically challenged. His short stature prompted him to climb a tree just to get a glimpse of Jesus. The fact that his stature is mentioned in the text probably indicates that his size had been a point of derision. Two other facts about Zacchaeus tell us he was not a popular man: he was a tax collector and he was rich. Since, he had used his tax office to his own advantage, it is unlikely that he had many friends.

I am sure that those lining the parade route to catch a glimpse of Jesus were startled when Jesus singled out Zacchaeus and invited Himself to stay in his home. Look at the response of Zacchaeus: "And he hurried and came down and received Him gladly" (Luke 19:6). Who would have thought that Zacchaeus would have been so responsive to the Gospel? None of the townspeople, that's for sure. In fact, they complained about Jesus lodging with a sinful man. What they failed to see is that the Father is already at work in the life of

Zacchaeus. Zacchaeus is so needy that he risks being the brunt of derisive jokes about short people when he climbs the tree to see Jesus.

The formula is simple but effective. Ask the Father to show you where He is at work and then act in such a manner that you *Show People Love And Share Him*.

A Few Radical but Simple Ideas

• The first issue in *showing* is our personal lifestyle. Ask the Holy Spirit to produce His fruit in your life. Ask the Father to manifest His name in your life. Remember that your attitude and behavior will be the first evidence of the Gospel and will provide many opportunities for sharing.

• Ask the Father to show you where He is working to advance His kingdom. Look for the needy person and ask God to open a door for you to *show* Jesus' love to that person.

• To show love, you must first see people. Look at people around you. What do you see? Do you see a needy woman standing alone at the well or a sinner to be shunned and avoided. Do you see a diminutive man who has long been the brunt of the community jokes or a despised tax collector who preys upon people?

• You may find it helpful to ask yourself the age old question—"What would Jesus do?"

• Show that you see people by asking them appropriate questions. For example, if you see a foreigner you might ask, "Where are you from? Do you need any help?"

These questions might open a door of opportunity for you to show love.

- Don't underestimate the power of appropriate touch. When Jesus touched the leper, embraced the little children or allowed the woman with an issue of blood to touch Him, His touch showed love. When you put a hand on a grieving friend's shoulder or express appropriate tenderness to someone who feels alone, you show love.

Reflections

- What do the stories we studied this week have in common?

_____

_____

_____

_____

_____

- What factors in the behavior of Jesus opened the door for further conversation about the Gospel?

_____

_____

_____

_____

SPLASH Show People Love And Share Him

- Thinking back on your life, name some persons who showed the Gospel to you. What did they do?

- Can you think about a time recently that you missed an opportunity to show the Gospel to someone? What happened?

- Share about a time when your actions showed the Gospel.

Assignment

Think through the week to come. What are you prepared to do to show the Gospel to someone?

PEOPLE

The address on the visitor's card told me that our "prospect" lived in a prestigious neighborhood in Virginia Beach. Accompanied by one of our deacons, I was making our standard follow-up visit to persons who visited our church. When I drove into the driveway, saw the size of the home, and noticed the manicured lawn, I knew this was no routine visit. Our church was made up of salt-of-the-earth, working-class people. We had grown quickly because of the willingness of people to serve, but we were always struggling financially because of the income level of our folks.

I was thinking to myself that this guy could surely solve some of our money problems if he joined our church. I actually think I verbalized something to that effect to my deacon partner. As I was completing my comment concerning the "prospect" we were preparing to visit, a voice from the porch shattered my dreams of a balanced budget. "Good evening pastor, we've been anticipating your visit!" He had been standing in a darkened area on the porch awaiting our visit and in my haste to sign him up for church and recruit him for our budget committee, I had not even noticed him standing in the shadows.

I must confess that my first fear was that he had overheard my callous remark. My second was that we would lose a valuable prospect. It was at that moment the Holy Spirit convicted me of seeing this man as a "prospect" and not a person in need. I had to ask myself, "Am I visiting this man based on what he can do for our church or because he is a person of value to the Father and a person with spiritual needs?"

Evangelism is not about prospects but about people. The question is not what a person can do for our church or for us, but what Christ has done and can do for them. If we are going to *Splash* people with Living Water, we must first see them as individuals created in God's image.

Jesus had both the ability and compassion to see persons for who they are and who they can become. We are often guilty of seeing crowds but not people. We are guilty of seeking out people for what they can do for us and not because of their inherent value. Jesus saw people both from the standpoint of their need and their potential. He sees what people can be when released from their sin and their past failures.

The calling of the disciples is a case in point. Luke tells us that the crowds press in so closely to hear Jesus teach that He is forced to commandeer Simon's boat for a floating pulpit. When He finishes speaking, He rewards the fisherman's generosity by taking him on a fishing trip.

If you think that it sounds strange for a preacher to invite a professional fisherman out on a fishing trip, you are not alone. Peter is dubious about any possibility for a catch since they had fished all night with no results.

He considered fishing during the heat of the sun a tiring and unproductive task.

Nonetheless Peter is so taken by this man who would meet him on his turf that he obeys. You may know the rest of the story. The catch of fish is so abundant that Peter recognizes the authority of Jesus—this is no ordinary man. He begs Jesus to go away because he knows himself to be a sinful man. But Jesus has no intention of leaving. He has seen more than a crude fisherman; he sees a man who has the potential to be a great fisher of men (Luke 5:1-11).

The calling of Levi, also known as Matthew, is another illustration of how Jesus focuses on the person. Here is how Luke tells the story: "After that He went out and noticed a tax collector named Levi sitting in the tax booth, and He said to him, 'Follow Me.' And he left everything behind, and got up and began to follow Him" (Luke 5:27-28).

You have probably surmised that tax collectors were not on any popularity list in Jesus' day. Rome farmed out the taxing system regionally, and the taxes in this area were paid to Herod Antipas. Most tax collectors abused the system to line their own pockets, and thus, Levi, like Zacchaeus, would have been viewed by most as a collaborator with Rome and an opportunist. I am certain that this despised tax collector was surprised that Jesus would select him to be in his inner circle of followers. When we look at the entire list of the early disciples, we are reminded that Jesus saw need, and He saw potential.

In Luke 8, we discover another group of people whom Jesus sees both for their need and their potential. They are simply referred to as "some women." Women were not always included in ministry assignments in Jesus' day. In fact, a rabbi (teacher) would not speak to a woman in public. Each woman included in the "some women" category has been healed by Jesus. Mary Magdalene is one of the few women who is actually named. She stands out because of her tremendous need. She had been possessed of seven demons. Not only did Jesus deliver her of the demons, he also called her to be His follower. Mary became a supporter of Jesus' ministry.

Matthew 9:36 provides a wonderful summary statement for the ministry of Jesus: "Seeing the people, He felt compassion for them, because they were distressed and dispirited like sheep without a shepherd." When Jesus saw people, He saw their pain and their hopelessness. Sheep without a shepherd are helpless and hopeless. Do you believe that people without Jesus are helpless and hopeless? Until we understand the disastrous consequences of sin, we will continue to see crowds and not persons.

A Few Suggestions to Draw People to Jesus

Always have bait handy. I was making an early morning trip to the airport and in a desperate attempt to stay awake, I began channel surfing the radio to find an interesting talk show. I settled on a program where an interview was being conducted with a man who made his living as a "crappie" fishing guide.

Yes, people make their living taking other people to catch "crappie."

I am aware that this sounds like a pretty boring topic to a man who doesn't fish. And I don't! But the truth is it was rather fascinating. This elderly gentleman talked with authority. In fact, I quickly became convinced that he knew more about "crappie" than the fish knew about each other. He discussed their habits like he had been swimming with them. He explained the various baits that needed to be employed to catch this particular variety of fish in different climatic conditions. He recommended buying several of each of these lures so the fisherman would be prepared in every circumstance. In conclusion, he insisted that anyone serious about catching "crappie" would never leave their home without their rod and reel and a well-stocked fishing tackle box. He declared that you could just never tell when and where the "crappie" would be biting. The serious fisherman is always prepared.

This entertaining interview quickly became for me a convicting message from the Holy Spirit. If I am serious about "fishing" for men, I need to know more about the "people" I am trying to catch. But the most convicting issue for me came from the story about the well-stocked tackle box. I realized that I often left home without any "lures" that I could use to "make a splash" for Christ. I began to carry tracts and other kinds of spiritual lures that would assist me to Show People Love and Share Him.

It was not long before I was prompted to write the series of little books called "Kingdom Promises" (see Appendix 2). I began to carry these little books in my tackle box. I had discovered that people might refuse a tract but they will accept a little book because it has perceived value. Now I regularly "cast" these books into the waters where I think "people" may be receptive to the Gospel.

I give them to waitresses, flight attendants, and new friends I meet along the way. One time at a restaurant, I was being seated by a hostess who was a lovely Indian lady. I asked her if she had recently moved from India. She responded with a lovely smile and an enthusiastic "yes." I asked her if she was a Hindu and the response was equally enthusiastic. I told her that I was a Christian and then asked her if she was curious about the identity of Jesus. I will never forget her response— "We all are!" Then I asked if she would be interested in reading a little book that told her about Jesus. Her positive response was followed by several "thank yous" when I gave her the *He Is* book.

Be Approachable. We can read a text so many times that we overlook an important detail. Matthew 8:2a gives us an important clue to Jesus' effectiveness in ministry that could be missed: "And a leper came to Him and bowed down before Him." Right away a man with a serious skin disease came up and knelt before Him. A leper approached Jesus! Lepers didn't approach anyone. They were prohibited from doing so. Leprosy was considered to be a contagious disease, and lepers were outcasts who were forced to live in leper colonies. When they saw someone approaching, they would cry out, "Unclean, unclean!" The leper not only came because he believed Jesus *could* help him, he came because he believed Jesus *would* help him. Do people ever approach you for a ministry need? If not, why not?

When we observe the life and ministry of Jesus, we are constantly reminded that people were drawn to Him. Children wanted to be around Him. A woman with an issue of blood would brave the ridicule of the crowd to grab His garment. The blind and lame sought Him out. Rulers and centurions desired His assistance. Why? Because they were needy, and He was approachable! They were drawn to Him because they had seen the clear evidence that He genuinely cared about people. When people observe that we genuinely care about them, they will be drawn to Christ in us.

Let's think together about a few examples. Do you call the waitress or the waiter in a restaurant by name? Do you ask their name if they don't have a name tag? What about the clerk at the register in the grocery store? Or your mailman? Do you reach out to the people in your sphere of influence?

Here again is where "having bait" is effective. I was in the Atlanta airport when I sensed that the "fish might be biting." A Delta employee looked harassed as she explained to another irate customer why the plane would be delayed. I walked up and could read her thought—"I can't handle one more complaint." I addressed her with a smile and indicated that I thought she could use a little promise from God. I handed her the Kingdom Promise book entitled *But God*. She wept as she declared "God must have sent you today."

I have regularly given the Kingdom Promise books to people I meet where I work out and play golf. The other day one of them called out to me, thanking me for the little book and declaring what an impact it had made in his life. Fill your tackle box with any bait you think might help you catch men and women for Christ. Make a cast and trust God to give the results.

Put People's Needs over Regulations and Institutions. As I reread the gospels while writing this material, I was surprised to notice how frequently Jesus' healing miracles occurred on the Sabbath. Yet as I thought about it, it made perfectly good sense. People who are in need would naturally gravitate to a place where religious people, who might take pity on them, would be gathered. Tragically, they must have often been disappointed by the callousness of those who were in charge of the synagogues and Temple in their day. Most of the religious leaders were more concerned with preserving the institution and obeying regulations than with meeting the needs of those who came seeking help.

Does this sound familiar? Are we sometimes more concerned about maintaining a building or preserving a traditional way of doing things at church than we are about meeting people's needs? I once spent the night in a major southern city. It was a Saturday night, and I wasn't preaching the next day. I discovered that there was a large evangelical church only blocks from my hotel. I arrived in time for Sunday school only to discover the front doors were locked. After trying several entry points, I turned to leave. An elderly church member chased me down the street, inviting me to come around to the back where there was an open door. I suggested that he might want to inform someone the front doors were locked. Without hesitation, he responded, "Oh, we have to keep those doors locked to keep the needy out." I'm sure the church was inundated with the "homeless," but I was nonetheless grieved by a strategy that would keep the "needy" out.

Jesus was headed to Jerusalem for a Jewish festival. On his way, He encountered a man who had been lying by the Pool of Bethesda for thirty-eight years, hoping to be healed by the waters believed to have curative power. Jesus posed a curious question, "Do you wish to get well?" (John 5:6). The man's response is pitiful. He indicated that he had no one to help him into the pool.

Have you ever considered how many people on their way to worship in Jerusalem had passed this man without ever asking about his need or offering to help? They were so focused on their religious responsibility to fulfill the Sabbath requirements and their own issues that they couldn't see the obvious needs around them. Jesus healed the man and told him to roll up his bedroll and walk. When the Jews saw the man carrying his bedroll, they expressed no joy at his healing. They simply declared that it was illegal for him to carry his bedroll on the Sabbath.

On another occasion Jesus was teaching in one of the local synagogues on the Sabbath. A woman was present who had been disabled for eighteen years (Luke 13:10-17). Jesus healed the woman with a caring touch, and she immediately began to glorify God. This is what the synagogue and the Sabbath should be about, right? The leader of the synagogue quoted Genesis, declaring that six days are enough time for one's labor. Jesus rebuked the leader by indicating that any one of them would untie his ox or donkey and lead it to water on the Sabbath. In other words, they showed more compassion for their animals than they did for people. That hits a little close to home, doesn't it? I see people who are far more concerned about the welfare of a stray pet than they are for the lost in their community.

You may remember that the Pharisees rebuked Jesus for allowing His disciples to pluck grain on the Sabbath. Jesus reminded them that David ate the sacred bread, which was reserved for the priests. He then declared that the Son of Man is Lord of the Sabbath and that He desired mercy and not sacrifice (Matthew 12:1-8). The Sabbath was created to meet man's needs, not to place a legalistic burden on man. God is concerned about the welfare of His people.

Are we so concerned with "running the church" that we are tempted to forget why it was established in the first place—to meet needs and reach the lost? I once heard of a church that made it clear "kids" from the community were not welcome. They were afraid that they might mark up the halls with their wild antics. One self righteous member simply declared, "These kids just don't know how to act in church." The church is a hospital and not a museum. We should be touching lives, not preserving sacred traditions.

When Jesus forgave the woman taken in the act of adultery, He put her spiritual condition above the desire of the legalists who wanted Him to participate in her stoning. He not only offered forgiveness; He warned her about the dire consequences of future sin. Jesus' concern was for her deepest need. Do we manifest more concern for our institutions and regulations than we do for people? If we are forced to answer "yes" to this question, we may have put our finger on the reason for our inability to reach and minister to those living all around us.

Look for Those Who Seem to be Invisible. Jesus drew people to Himself like a magnet draws metal filings. Many of those persons would have been "invisible" to their neighbors. You remember the story of Zacchaeus the tax collector. He was probably the brunt of jokes because of his size, but he was certainly despised because of his profession. He worked for the hated Romans and took advantage of his neighbors. Who wanted to be seen with a man like this? Jesus did!

Matthew tells the story of a Canaanite mother from the region of Tyre and Sidon who persisted in following Jesus crying out for Jesus to have mercy on her daughter. This mother was desperate! Her daughter was tormented by a demon. Jesus' own disciples were embarrassed by the woman's loud outbursts. "Send her away, because she keeps shouting at us" (Matthew 15:23c). The disciples are clearly embarrassed by the behavior of this woman. They wished that she would simply disappear. Perhaps they would have been more patient if she had been a Jew instead of a Gentile. Rather than send her away, Jesus acknowledges the woman's faith and cures her daughter.

The list of culturally invisible persons to whom Jesus ministered would include lepers, widows, fallen women, women in general, children, tax collectors, known sinners, political leaders, and even religious leaders. I know you are thinking that surely children can't be in that list; everyone loves children. Mark tells us that some people were bringing their children to Jesus so that He might touch them. Guess who wants to turn them away? Right, again! It is the disciples, the intimate group of followers whom Jesus had chosen to carry on His ministry (Mark 10:13-16). I find that I am quick to put people into categories and then avoid those who make me most uncomfortable. Yet, when I read about the ministry of Jesus, I am convicted. I learn that it is precisely those persons who were the most receptive to Jesus' message of hope and spiritual healing.

The reaction of the disciples to the "invisible people" hits too close to home for us to ignore, doesn't it? "Those kids from the projects just won't fit in here. We don't want those skater kids at our church; they will be a disruptive influence. Those people living in the trailer park wouldn't feel comfortable here." But this book really isn't about the church reaching out; it is about you reaching out. Who can you think of in your sphere of influence, "your *splash zone*," that you often overlook, either intentionally or unintentionally?

Jesus was effective at meeting the needs of those the world ignored, the invisible, because He saw valuable individuals. After all, Jesus said the physician came for those needing a doctor, not for those who think they are well. Are we sensitive to the hurting and invisible people in our neighborhood, at work, or at school? Or are we drawn only to those who already have their act together?

Do the Unexpected. Jesus was a master of the unexpected act of kindness. This is precisely how He splashed people with Living Water. He openly speaks to the scorned Samaritan woman. He even asked for her assistance, thus treating her with respect. He invited Himself to the home of Zacchaeus. The joyous response of Zacchaeus tells us how truly lonely he was. Jesus allowed a prostitute to wash His feet with her tears and dry them with her hair (Luke 7:36-50). He physically touched a leper and allowed Himself to be touched by a woman with a chronic illness. He invited "some women" into His inner circle of followers (Luke 8:1-3). Over and over, Jesus did the unexpected act of tenderness. He validated these individuals' worth.

Mark tells us of a remarkable event that was such an unexpected act of kindness that it contributed to the betrayal of Jesus. Everything about the event is extraordinary. Jesus was at the home of Simon, the leper. This one fact alone was shocking but then Jesus allows a woman to pour expensive oil on His head. We are told that some guests were incensed that the oil was wasted. They thought it could have been sold and the receipts given to the poor. It appears that this unexpected act of kindness tipped the scales for Judas who then determined to betray Jesus. He must have been thinking that no one so kind and gentle could be the conquering King (Mark 14:3-11).

But Jesus was and is the King of Kings and Lord of Lords and He drew people to His kingdom by seeing them as individuals in need of a King who offered acceptance, forgiveness, and wholeness. Today people will be drawn to our King when we allow Him to demonstrate His love through us.

You Must See People and Have Compassion on Them. Matthew 9:35 serves as a summary statement of the "people-centered" strategy of Jesus. "Jesus was going through all the cities and villages, teaching in their synagogues and proclaiming the Gospel of the kingdom, and healing every kind of disease and every kind of sickness." What compelled Him to face the grueling task of moving from town to town? Matthew provides the answer: "Seeing the people, He felt compassion for them, because they were distressed and dispirited like sheep without a shepherd" (9:36).

Compassion comes from a proper understanding of the condition of the lost and the passion of the Good Shepherd to meet their needs. People who do not know Christ are like sheep without a shepherd. Not moved yet? Do you fully comprehend the condition of sheep whose shepherd leaves them alone? They are bear bait! Sheep must have a shepherd to protect and care for them.

On another occasion, Jesus tells a parable about a shepherd who had a hundred sheep and discovered that one was missing. This shepherd, without delay, leaves the ninety-nine to search for the lost sheep. He knew it could not survive the night alone. Do you fully understand that persons without Christ are like lost sheep in danger? They are in danger of spending eternity in hell, separated forever from the presence of God. As you encounter people, do you believe the Good Shepherd can and will use you as He meets their every need? Here is a promise that will encourage you to *splash* a little Living Water on everyone you meet: "The Lord is not slow about His promise, as some count slowness, but is patient toward you, not wishing for any to perish but for all to come to repentance" (2 Peter 3:9). Just ask the Father to help you see people with His eyes and to feel with His heart. Ask Him to give you the confidence to believe He is sufficient for every situation.

Questions to Ponder

• Do I see people as they are, or do I see them for who they can be in Christ?

_____

_____

_____

_____

_____

• Do I tend to group people into artificial categories and ignore those who make me uncomfortable?

_____

_____

_____

_____

- When have I been guilty of putting institutions and regulations above people?

- Am I approachable? What can I do to be more approachable?

- What unexpected act of kindness can I do that will minister to someone this week?

• Am I willing to ask God to give me a heart of compassion for the needs of the people around me?

Reflections

• What led Jesus to select the men and women who became His intimate followers?

• What did Jesus see in us that would cause Him to give His life for us?

SPLASH SHOW PEOPLE LOVE AND SHARE HIM

- In your opinion, why did Jesus see people whom others often overlooked?

_____

_____

_____

_____

_____

- Who are the "invisible people" in your *splash zone*? Each person has various areas in his/her splash zone. Your family and relatives are your closest zone. Your neighbors are your next zone, then your colleagues at work, etc. Who are you thinking of right now?

_____

_____

_____

_____

Assignment

In Appendix 4 is a chart to help you to think through your *splash zone*. Before you begin his/her next reading assignment, place the name of at least one person in each *splash zone* on the diagram.

LOVE

Denise wanted to share her faith story with her brother and his football player buddies. Denise knew that the quickest way to a man's heart is through his stomach, so she invited the boys over for a home-cooked meal. She was up front about her intentions. She would feed them if they would let her share the most important thing in life—her relationship to Jesus Christ. Denise knew the guys might have questions so she also included Pastor Ed in the invitation.

The night came and Denise prepared a great meal. After dinner, she shared her love for Christ and told how Jesus forgave her sins and healed her heart of past hurts. Pastor Ed answered questions honestly and openly for the guys.

Denise modeled the biblical story of Jesus' disciple Levi, also called Matthew (Luke 5:27-39). When Matthew followed Jesus, he wanted his friends to meet the man who changed his life and could change theirs too. He hosted a big party, a reception at his house. Hospitality opened the door for Jesus to teach and share with Matthew's friends. Denise treated her brother and his friends with love. She prepared her home for them to hear the good news.

SPLASH Show People Love And Share Him

Perhaps you have heard the song with the lyrics, "What the world needs now is love, sweet love, it's the only thing that there's just too little of." That was the theme song of a generation calling for a kinder and gentler world. I'm not sure how authentic or practical this call for love was, but we would probably all agree that the world could use more love.

My dad was a wonderful storyteller. I remember a story he told about a recalcitrant young man who was always in trouble with the principal. The principal attempted every form of discipline he could think of to change the behavior of the teen before he graduated from high school. The principal was sitting in his office one day when a frustrated teacher appeared with the young man in tow.

In sheer frustration, the principal said to the young man, "What am I to do with you? I have tried everything I know with no results. I've required you to stay after school. I've had the teachers assign extra work, and I've even expelled you. Nothing seems to matter to you. What do you think I should do?"

The principal's final question was probably intended to be rhetorical, but the young man took the opportunity to answer the principal's plea. "You could try to love me," he sobbed. "No one has ever loved me."

The principal was shaken. He never dreamed that this hardened teen might actually respond to love. Was it possible this teenager had never experienced genuine love? He concluded that this young man's unruly behavior had been a cry for attention, a cry for love. Genuine love breaks down walls of resistance and

42

prepares people to hear the good news that God loves them even in their sin and rebellion.

God is Love

"Love Him, love Him, all you little children, God is love, God is love." As a child, I loved to sing this little chorus. God is love! To say that God is love sounds simple and childlike, and yet it is a profound biblical truth that defines the very character of God.

John, in his first letter, calls his readers to love one another based on the singular truth—God is love:

> Beloved, let us love one another, for love is from God; and everyone who loves is born of God and knows God. The one who does not love does not know God, for God is love. By this the love of God was manifested in us, that God sent His only begotten Son into the world so that we might live through Him... We have come to know and have believed the love which God has for us. God is love, and the one who abides in love abides in God, and God abides in him" (1 John 4:7-9, 16).

There is probably no verse that is more cherished than John 3:16: "For God so loved the world, that He gave His only begotten Son, that whoever believes in Him shall not perish, but have eternal life." Can you imagine a love so great that the Father would send His Son to die in your place? Paul places God's great love in its proper perspective when he declares: "But God demonstrates His own love toward us, in that while we were yet sinners, Christ died for us" (Romans 5:8).

God sent His Son to die for us in spite of our rebellion and our sin.

The Pharisees always tried to find a way to trick Jesus into saying something that would be considered blasphemous. On one occasion, an expert in the law asked Jesus which commandment in the law is the greatest. Jesus' reply silenced them: "'YOU SHALL LOVE THE LORD YOUR GOD WITH ALL YOUR HEART, AND WITH ALL YOUR SOUL, AND WITH ALL YOUR MIND.' This is the great and foremost commandment. The second is like it, 'YOU SHALL LOVE YOUR NEIGHBOR AS YOURSELF.' On these two commandments depend the whole Law and the Prophets" (Matthew 22:37-40). Jesus is clearly declaring that "love" is at the very core of all biblical teaching and, thus, is to be characteristic of those who love God. But, notice the connection between the two commandments. When we truly love God, we will, in turn, love our neighbor. Our love for others flows out of God's love for us.

It is significant that Jesus, as He prepares His disciples for His departure, indicates that love will characterize the life of those who follow Him. After washing His disciples' feet, Jesus declares, "A new commandment I give to you, that you love one another, even as I have loved you, that you also love one another. By this all men will know that you are My disciples, if you have love for one another" (John 13:34-35). After telling His disciples that He is the vine and they are branches, Jesus indicates that He loved them in the same manner that the Father loved Him. Now He issues and repeats a single command. "This is My commandment, that you love one another, just as I have loved you" (John 15:12 and cf. 15:17).

Love is not optional for the Christian. It is a command. It is the evidence that we have experienced God's love in Christ Jesus. Could it be that those who find it difficult to love others have never experienced the love of God? If you sometimes struggle to love those difficult people in your splash zone, focus on deepening your relationship with Christ. He will love people through you.

Love is Not Just a Feeling

We have another problem when it comes to love. Often we define love only in terms of a feeling. I have counseled troubled husbands and wives who contemplated divorce. Their reason: "I just don't love him/her anymore." When we talk about falling "into" and "out" of love, we fortify this false notion of love as little more than a chemical reaction producing an emotional high. If we are going to show people "love," we must first understand that love will produce action; it will cause us to demonstrate the reality of our affection. Love is first and foremost an act of the will—a choice.

No passage is more quoted or read in wedding ceremonies than 1 Corinthians 13. It is sometimes called "the hymn to love." Paul did not write this passage as a sentimental hymn to love. It was a critical corrective to the exaggerated spirituality of some in the Corinthian community who believed that certain spiritual gifts proved their "advanced spirituality." He begins 1 Corinthians 13 with the declaration that one can abound in spectacular gifts such as prophecy and miracle-working faith and still be a spiritual zero.

Later Paul declares, "Love is patient, love is kind and is not jealous; love does not brag and is not arrogant, does not act unbecomingly; it does not seek its own, is not provoked, does not take into account a wrong suffered, does not rejoice in unrighteousness, but rejoices with the truth; bears all things, believes all things, hopes all things, endures all things" (13:4-7). The parallels with the fruit of the Spirit are too obvious to ignore. Love is the character of God produced in our lives by the Holy Spirit. Our expression of love must be active and long-suffering. It will produce kind actions. It will not keep a list of wrongs suffered. Love will endure in all circumstances.

In Romans 12, Paul has just completed discussing spiritual gifts when once again he speaks on the centrality of love: "Let love be without hypocrisy. Abhor what is evil; cling to what is good. Be devoted to one another in brotherly love; give preference to one another in honor" (Romans 12:9-10). Love is addressed in practical terms. The person expressing love clings to good and zealously places the needs of another before his own. Paul is not finished talking about the practical nature of love. He mentions issues such as practicing hospitality (13), blessing when persecuted (14), celebrating the accomplishments of others and sharing their grief (15), associating with the humble (16), and doing good to your enemy (20). Paul encourages us to overcome evil with good (21). The actions Paul lists here are not what we usually speak of when we are thinking about evangelistic opportunities, but they often provide the best means of splashing people with a little Living Water.

When an expert in the law wants to know what he must do to inherit eternal life, Jesus simply asks him what the law says about the matter. The lawyer responds correctly by quoting the two commandments on loving God and loving your neighbor (Luke 10:27). After Jesus tells him that he must actually embody these two commandments, the lawyer attempts to excuse himself by asking, "And who is my neighbor?" (Luke 10:29b).

Jesus responds by telling the story of the Good Samaritan whose actions stand in stark contrast to the indifference of the priest and the Levite. The priest and the Levite saw the man in need and passed right by him. The Samaritan not only saw the injured man; but he also had compassion on him. He bandaged the man's wounds, took him to an inn, and paid for his care. Love is always expressed in action.

The message of love in action flows throughout Scripture, but perhaps the most challenging summary is found in 1 John 3:16-18:

> We know love by this, that He laid down His life for us; and we ought to lay down our lives for the brethren. But whoever has the world's goods, and sees his brother in need and closes his heart against him, how does the love of God abide in him? Little children, let us not love with word or with tongue, but in deed and truth.

It is our own experience of God's love that motivates us to respond to the needs of others with loving actions.

But it is not enough to say that God's love elicits our love. Look closer at the text. God's love becomes the model for our love. We come to know love because God laid down His life for us and now we are called to lay down our lives for our brothers. John then makes a real-life application. If we see someone in need and do not respond with compassion, does God's love actually resides in us? We cannot simply claim that we are loving people; we must express our love in concrete actions.

Love the Least Lovely

The context of several of the passages discussed in this section indicates that the biblical authors were dealing primarily with loving actions within the Christian community. Yet, it is clearly the concern of Scripture for love to be the distinguishing mark of those who are God's children. It is therefore not surprising that Paul ends the discussion of love in Romans 12 with a mandate for believers to do good to their enemies. We can overcome evil with good! Love's overcoming power will provide the bridge that will enable us to share Him.

Immediately after calling out the twelve apostles, Jesus discusses the broad scope of love that will be characteristic of His followers: "But I say to you who hear, love your enemies, do good to those who hate you, bless those who curse you, pray for those who mistreat you" (Luke 6:27-28). Nothing is left to sentimental speculation. He speaks about turning the other cheek when abused, giving your shirt when someone takes your coat, and willingly giving to those who take advantage of you. Jesus then asks a penetrating question: "If you love those who love you, what credit is that to you?" (32a). He declares that even sinners love those who love them. When we love our enemies, we express the character of our Father who is gracious to the ungrateful and the evil. Christians are called to be merciful like their Father.

It is the love of God expressed in Christ Jesus that causes us to abandon our sin and seek God's mercy. In the same way, it will be the love of God expressed through us that will draw people to the Master. When we begin to love with radical abandon, we will discover avenues for sharing Him we never saw before. Such unselfish behavior is so counter-cultural in our world where "looking-out-for-number-one" is the byword of the day that your life will function like salt, creating a thirst for the Gospel.

What would happen to those difficult people in your splash zone if you determined to love them the way Jesus loved His enemies? Do you think they would be drawn to Christ? It's certainly a radical idea, but I think it is a biblical one.

Learn from the Master

Jesus' entire ministry was defined by the demonstration of love. We could think of the story of the woman at the well. She was shunned by the "respectable" women of the day. She had already gone through five husbands and was living unlawfully with a man who was not her husband. Yet, Jesus spoke to her in a public place, asked her to draw water for Him, and treated her with tenderness even as He exposed her sin. It would be wonderful to know the full content of their discussion at the well. From the woman's reaction, it is obvious that she knew she had encountered a man who looked at her with love and not lust, a man who knew who she was but gave her the hope that she could be more.

We are overwhelmed by the love required for Jesus to reach out and touch a leper. We are impressed by the deep emotions elicited at the death of His dear friend Lazarus. We are surprised and moved when He chooses to invite Himself to the home of a tax-collector. We are overwhelmed with Jesus' kindness as He allows a fallen woman to wash His feet with her tears and wipe them with her hair. Jesus expresses the love of God with concrete acts of kindness.

No event more clearly depicts a concrete expression of love than the encounter with the woman who was brought before Him for committing adultery. As we examine this text again, we see that it seems to suggest that the woman has been caught in the very act of adultery (John 8:3). It makes you wonder if the whole event was a "set up" designed only to entrap Jesus. In any case, it is apparent that the scribes and Pharisees have no regard for the woman as they make her stand in the middle of the crowd in the temple complex. Some commentators suggest she may have been dragged from the bed and, thus, would have stood fully exposed before the crowd of men.

The legalists want Jesus to sentence her to death by stoning. Jesus' response is disarming. He begins to write in the dirt. We have no record of what He wrote, but it is clear that all eyes are now on Him and not the exposed woman. When they continue to question Him about the matter, He simply tells them that the one without sin should throw the first stone. Jesus continues writing on the ground until everyone leaves. He is left alone with the woman. He expresses tenderness as He declares that He does not condemn her. His love is not mere sentimentality. He warns her to abandon sin (John 8:11).

Expressions of Love

How do we move from theory to practice? How can we show people love in such a manner that we gain the right to share Him? First, we must confess that radical love can only be manifested in us through the ministry of the Holy Spirit who desires to produce the fruit of the Spirit in and through us. Ask the Father to fill you with His Spirit. Second, we must see people through the eyes of Jesus. Each day, we must ask God to show us those who need His love. Further, we must commit to do whatever it takes to love people to Christ.

Can you think of any concrete actions you can take? When my wife was undergoing cancer treatment, a woman we barely knew sent a basket full of small gifts with instructions for Paula to open one a day. Each gift was accompanied by a verse of Scripture. You cannot imagine how much this small expression of love lifted our spirits. What if you did this for a non-Christian friend who was going through a difficult time?

Send a card of encouragement or buy a small gift for someone. Offer to take a friend to the doctor and volunteer to sit in the waiting room with them. Volunteer at the cancer center, coach little league, become a big brother or big sister, babysit for free for a young couple, mow the grass for a shut-in, or invite a neighbor in for coffee and listen to them.

"Home is where the heart is." Home is also where *Splashing* should be the most natural and the most fun. Jesus often taught valuable lessons around the table while eating with His disciples and their friends. The word "companion" comes from two root words that mean "with bread." A companion is one with whom we break bread—we share the best of life over food and fellowship.

Biblical hospitality is welcoming strangers into God's presence. God is the perfect host. He sets a table for us when we need comfort (Psalm 23:5). Jesus models hospitality for all disciples. He promises to prepare a place for us (John 14: 2-3). Before His death, Jesus hosts his disciples for the Last Supper. He washes their feet and serves them (John 13). After His resurrection, Jesus fixed breakfast for these men beside the Sea of Galilee (John 21:9-14).

Who could you invite home to meet Jesus? Here are a few of many easy ways to host a party with a purpose.

- Host a Christmas coffee or a brunch for your neighbors. On the invitation make a note– "We will share the Christmas story." Keep it simple! After fellowship and food, tell the nativity story from Luke 2 or have a friend read the story and then share what it means to you and your family.

- Invite the neighborhood children to a birthday party for Jesus the week before Christmas. Have a birthday cake and goodies. Before cutting the cake, share the story of Jesus' birth. If you desire, give each child an age appropriate gift. Explain that God's gift of His Son is the reason for gift giving at Christmas.
- Share an Easter egg hunt and picnic with friends and their families. Ask everyone to bring a dish to share. Before the meal, share the biblical story of the first Easter. For the egg hunt, fill plastic eggs with scripture verses as well as treats. You might want to have eggs with prize numbers and give away Bible story books as prizes.

Every time you express God's love for another, you are splashing a little Living Water on them.

Reflections

As you read the Gospel accounts, what do you find unique in the love of God as expressed in the life of Jesus?

_____

_____

_____

_____

_____

SPLASH Show People Love And Share Him

In your opinion, which story in the gospels most clearly demonstrates God's love to you? Why?

_____

_____

_____

_____

_____

Read Romans 12:9-21. List the concrete expressions of love Paul enumerates.

_____

_____

_____

_____

_____

How do these actions provide an opportunity to share Him?

_____

_____

_____

_____

_____

In your small group, list ideas of other actions to express God's love?

_____

_____

_____

_____

_____

Assignment

In our last session you identified persons in your splash zone. What concrete action will you take this week to *splash* love on someone in need? Be prepared to share the results with the group next week.

AND

*"Having so fond an affection for you, we were
well pleased to impart to you not only
the gospel of God but also our own lives,
because you had become very dear to us."*
1 Thessalonians 2:8

Dawn's mother Judi was suffering a potentially terminal illness when we first met in the 1980s. Ken and I visited the family and offered our help personally and as a church family. We lived out that commitment to show love and share Him over the next twenty-plus years with Dawn.

Dawn was thirteen when her mother got sick. Multiple surgeries and hospitalizations followed for Judi. Dawn struggled to find her place as a teenager. She experimented with drugs, got into trouble at school, and was finally arrested for shop lifting. That afternoon she called and asked if I would come get her from the police station. She had assured me before that she was a Christian. As a young girl she had walked an aisle in her church and been baptized, but there was no evidence of Christ's joy or power in Dawn's life. The afternoon I picked Dawn up, we went back to our home and I asked Dawn again about her relationship with Christ. Very slowly and deliberately I shared Jesus' love and His desire to be Lord of Dawn's life. We knelt together and Dawn confessed her sin and asked Jesus to come into her heart! She was eighteen years old. Showing love prepared the way for sharing Christ.

Two years later her mother died and Dawn came to live with our family for eight months. She continued to struggle with eating disorders and drugs. Ken and I prayed for her deliverance and nurtured her in the faith. Once she told me she felt like a 13-year-old caught in a 20-year-old body. After leaving our home, Dawn bounced around from job to job and finally in 1998 she was arrested again for prescription drug fraud. During her subsequent jail time, Dawn began studying the Bible again and was finally drug free. Upon her release she began volunteering with other women coming out of jail. Today she continues to walk with the Lord and grow in her faith.

Showing love to a family in need opened a door of relationship with Dawn, but sharing Christ was intentional. Showing love took many forms. Discipline and tough love were combined with persistent prayer, material help, and persevering patience. Dawn has become very dear to us.

"Love and marriage, love and marriage, go together like a horse and carriage... You can't have one without the other." I can't remember the last time I heard this little tune. It is a bit old-fashioned, but the idea of a permanent commitment is certainly not old-fashioned. The song indicates that when a person is truly in love, commitment will lead to marriage. The little word "and" inextricably links love to marriage.

We don't pay much attention to little words like "and." We say them with such nonchalance that we hardly notice the hard work they do in a sentence. "And" is a conjunction that joins two equal parts. We use this little conjunction hundreds of times a day. Bread and butter. Toast and jam. Berries and cream. Fun and games. Field and stream. You get the idea.

This may be the shortest section of our study, but it is by no means the least important. It is about the conjunction of lifestyle and witness. It is the conjunction of salt and light. The first three chapters have demonstrated how Jesus showed people love. The last two will teach us how He shared Himself, how He shared the Gospel.

Like the song says, "We can't have one without the other." It borders on spiritual arrogance to say, "I share my witness by my life; I don't need to verbalize it." If Jesus felt it necessary to join lifestyle with verbal witness, we can do no less. We simply can't assume that people will understand why we are showing them love.

The *demonstration* of love prepares the way for the *articulation* of the Gospel. Loving deeds are like the gentle rain that softens the soil, making it receptive to the seed. We must also understand that a verbal witness that has no connection with a transformed lifestyle will seldom have much impact. Our friends and neighbors may have trouble hearing what we say because our actions, or lack thereof, create too much noise for them to hear our story.

Let's take our cue once again from the life of Jesus. He was and is the Master at showing people love and sharing Himself.

An Encounter at the Well

We have already looked briefly at the encounter with the Samaritan woman at the well near Sychar. She was drawn to Jesus because He treated her as a person of value. He spoke to her and even asked her to do Him a favor, but His splashes of kindness are accompanied by a verbal witness that stimulates interest and thus creates receptivity.

When Jesus asked her for a drink, she wanted to know why a Jewish man would ask a drink from a Samaritan woman (John 4:10). We must recall that in the context of her day, she had two strikes against her. She was a woman and a Samaritan. Jesus responded to her question in a manner that allowed Him to splash the woman with a little more Living Water. Listen to His reply: "Jesus answered and said to her, "If you knew the gift of God, and who it is who says to you, 'Give Me a drink,' you would have asked Him, and He would have given you living water" (4:10).

The woman is perplexed by Jesus' response and wants to know how He can draw water without a bucket. She then asks if Jesus thinks He is greater than Jacob who provided the wells. His response is designed to create a little more thirst for Living Water. Jesus tells her that whoever drinks from the water He provides will never thirst again (13-14). Do you see the multiple splashes of Living Water? First, Jesus treats her with unexpected kindness, causing her to see herself as a person of worth. Then, He allows her to do Him a favor and returns the favor by offering her the gift of Living Water. Next He enters into dialogue designed to create a thirst for this spiritual water.

When the woman responds that she wants the water He is offering, Jesus tells her to go get her husband. This command creates a crisis because she has been married five times and is now living with a man who is not her husband. Confronted with her sin, she attempts to change the tenor of the conversation by introducing a controversial issue. She wants to know who is right about the appropriate place of worship, the Jews or the Samaritans (4:20).

It is highly unlikely that the Samaritan woman had spent much time looking for a place of worship. She was simply trying to create a diversion and avoid the issue of her own sin. Jesus refuses to enter into speculation about the physical place of worship and instead points her to the Father and to Himself. We are often reluctant to share our faith story because we are afraid we can't answer all the objections of the skeptics. Notice that Jesus doesn't fall into the trap of debating theological issues such as the proper place of worship. Instead, He focuses on the woman's spiritual need. I have found that many "intellectual objections" are little more than a crafty maneuver to avoid the convicting power of the Holy Spirit. Follow Jesus' example and remain focused on the person and their spiritual need.

The woman finally confesses that she knows of the coming of the Messiah. Jesus' response is brief but pointed: "I who speak to you am He" (John 4:26b). Notice that loving action was joined with verbal explanation. Jesus shows her kindness and then He points her to Himself as the answer to her deepest need. When we show kindness, we must direct people to Jesus as the source of our kindness.

Thirty-Eight Years by the Pool

A lame man had been lying by the pool of Bethesda for thirty-eight years. He was waiting on the waters to be stirred so he could get into the famed "healing pool" and recover from his infirmity. One must wonder if he had grown comfortable with his lameness. Perhaps it was his infirmity that provided his income as persons passing by took pity on him. Is it possible that he became resigned to his lot in life? You will regularly meet people who have given up on life. They, too, assume that things will never improve.

Jesus began *splashing* healing water on him by first noticing him and then speaking to him (John 5:5-6). No doubt, this cripple had become such a fixture at this pool that many of those traveling to Jerusalem crossed to the other side of the pool to avoid eye contact. This is the same temptation we face when we encounter a beggar on the street corner. Others may have tossed a coin his way without pausing to speak, but Jesus saw him and spoke. Jesus' question was simple and to the point, "Do you wish to get well?"

When the man said "yes," Jesus commanded him to pick up his bedroll and walk. The physical cure was instant. The Jews were incensed that the lame man was audacious enough to carry his bedroll on the Sabbath, and they demanded to know who told him to break the Sabbath. The man indicated that he didn't know the identity of his benefactor.

In the next scene, we discover that Jesus sought the man out, finding him in the Temple complex. It is at this point that we find the "and" of the encounter. Jesus spoke to the man of his newfound health and told him to give up sinning: "Behold, you have become well; do not sin anymore, so that nothing worse happens to you" (5:14b). Jesus was not threatening the man or suggesting that his physical condition was the result of sin; He was simply telling Him that this physical life was not all there is. We are not privy to the entire conversation, but again, we can see the principle of incarnational evangelism followed by verbal explanation.

5000 Hungry Souls

We are not surprised to discover that huge crowds of people were drawn to Jesus. His life was such that people sought Him out. He was the Salt that gave life flavor. Some, no doubt, were simply curious, others were seeking truth, but all of them alike were needy. On one occasion, 5000 persons gathered to hear Him teach. As the day wore on, Jesus became concerned about the physical needs of the crowd. Out of His compassion, Jesus asked the disciples to provide food for them. You may recall that God provided an abundance of food from the five loaves and two fish given by a young lad (John 6:1-15).

The crowd was so moved by His generosity that they wanted to make Jesus their king. Jesus withdrew to the mountain to be alone with His Father. On the next day, the crowd followed Jesus to the other side of the Sea of Galilee. First, Jesus confronted the people for following only because they had eaten the loaves and been filled. In other words, they were looking for another handout. Now we see the "and" part of the process begin. Jesus used their hunger and their desire for food as the "conjunction" that allowed Him to explain the Gospel. He directed them from physical food that perishes to spiritual bread that lasts for eternity.

Jesus tells them, "For the bread of God is that which comes down out of heaven, and gives life to the world" (6:33). They respond by requesting this life-giving bread. "Jesus says, 'I am the bread of life; he who comes to Me will not hunger, and he who believes in Me will never thirst'" (6:35).

Jesus demonstrated the Gospel by providing physical food. Then He articulated the Gospel by pointing the hungry crowd to Himself as the spiritual bread which gives eternal life. Can you think of instances where you have made such a connection between an act of kindness and the kindness of the Lord?

An Adulteress Treated with Kindness and Forgiven

On several other occasions we examined the story of the woman caught committing adultery. We noticed the compassion and kindness with which Jesus treated this sinful woman. He drew on the ground, diverting attention from this exposed sinner. His statement—"I do not condemn you, either" (John 8:11b)—must have sounded like music to her ears. We must wonder how long she had felt the scorn and condemnation of those around her. When we demonstrate kindness rather than condemnation, we are preparing people and earning the right to share the Gospel.

There is an "and" to this story. Jesus tells the woman: "Go. From now on sin no more" (8:11c). Often, we want to be merciful without confronting the issue of sin that creates consequences in a person's life. Ignoring the sin problem is not a loving response. Jesus' ministry had the perfect balance of grace and truth, and He must be our model of *splashing* friends, enemies, and neighbors with the Gospel. The Gospel always contains a call for repentance. To release someone from a current problem and not offer them deliverance from sin is to stop short of delivering good news.

A Blind Man Regains His Sight

"As He passed by, He saw a man blind from birth. And His disciples asked Him, 'Rabbi, who sinned, this man or his parents, that he would be born blind?'" (John 9:1-2). What a revealing encounter! Jesus and His disciples see a blind man. The disciples see him and are prompted to raise theological questions about the relationship between sin and sickness. Jesus sees the man's need as the natural platform for God to reveal His mighty work. Listen to Jesus' perspective: "It (his blindness) was so that the works of God might be displayed in him" (9:3b). Do you believe that every need you encounter is a platform for God to reveal His mighty power?

Jesus healed the man of blindness, creating a stir among his neighbors who wonder if this is the same blind man who once sat begging. The "formerly" blind man answers with childlike simplicity: "The man who is called Jesus made clay, and anointed my eyes, and

65

said to me, 'Go to Siloam and wash'; so I went away and washed, and I received sight" (9:11b).

His friends bring him to the Pharisees who demand to know how he regained his sight. He repeats his simple story, and they insist on knowing who the blind man believes Jesus to be. He simply replies that he believes Jesus is a prophet. The doubting Pharisees call the man's parents to receive confirmation that he had been blind. The parents fear they will be expelled from the synagogue, and, thus, they declare that their son is of age and can speak for himself. The Pharisees want the formerly blind man to give glory to God and agree that Jesus is a sinner. I love the man's simple response: "Whether He is a sinner, I do not know; one thing I do know, that though I was blind, now I see" (9:25b). The Pharisees throw the man out because he refuses to vacillate in his testimony concerning Jesus.

It is at this juncture that we discover the "and" of the story. Listen to John's account of the encounter: "Jesus heard that they had put him out, and finding him, He said, 'Do you believe in the Son of Man?' He answered, 'Who is He, Lord, that I may believe in Him?' Jesus said to him, 'You have both seen Him, and He is the one who is talking with you.' And he said, 'Lord, I believe.' And he worshiped Him" (9:35-38).

We cannot assume that people will make the natural connection between our acts of kindness and the grace of God that prompts them. We must join salt to light, words to action, behavior to explanation. We must provide the conjunction between loving action and the loving Savior. If Jesus, who embodied the grace of God, sought out persons to explain to them the reason for His kindness, then we can do no less.

Reflections

Why did Jesus precede verbal witness with visual demonstration?

_____

_____

_____

_____

_____

How did Jesus intentionally transition from showing the Gospel to declaring the Gospel verbally?

_____

_____

_____

_____

Do you think Jesus would have been as effective in meeting people's needs if He had simply shown the Gospel? Why or why not?

_____

_____

_____

SPLASH Show People Love And Share Him

_____

_____

Your assignment last week was to perform an act of kindness for someone in one area of your *Splash Zone*. What did you do?

_____

_____

_____

_____

_____

What was the response?

_____

_____

_____

_____

Did you connect your action to a verbal witness? If not, how can you share Him verbally this week?

_____

_____

_____

_____

_____

Assignment

Choose an SEP. No, this is not an IRA or a rollover. An SEP is a Splash Effectiveness Partner. Your assignment before you leave class is to pray together for the people you have listed in your *Splash Zone*. Pray specifically for boldness to connect verbal witness to visual demonstration. Pray for an opportunity to share Him this week. You might want to call your partner by phone during the week for additional prayer and encouragement.

SHARE

Conduct yourselves with wisdom toward outsiders,
making the most of the opportunity.
Let your speech always be with grace, as though
seasoned with salt, so that you will know how you
should respond to each person.
Colossians 4:5-6

I sat alone in the small room at the Cancer Center waiting for my radiation treatment. A pretty young woman pushed an elderly gentleman in a wheelchair into the room and turned to leave. I immediately saw the large bandage on his head. It covered the spot to be targeted by the radiology technicians during treatment.

"Hi, my name is Paula. How are you feeling today?" I asked, trying to make conversation. "I'm George," he answered. "I'm not doing very well. This old tent of mine is folding and I'm ready to go home. Are you ready?" George asked me. I knew what he meant. George was prepared to die and he wanted to make sure I was ready when my time came. He was *splashing* me and *sharing* the hope of eternal life in a non-threatening way. I was thrilled to respond. "George, I am ready! I have followed Jesus since I was twelve years old and He gets sweeter every day!

I would like to stay here as long as the Lord wills and play with our grandbabies and take care of my husband Ken. When the time comes, though, I am ready."

George is the first person in my life who shared Jesus with me outside of a church building. He spoke of spiritual things when he had an opportunity. He asked a simple question. In the process he confronted me with my spiritual need for hope when life here comes to an end. He was comfortable asking and he made me comfortable answering.

I was in my first pastorate. The lady lying in the hospital bed was a pillar of the church and of the small rural community where I was called as pastor. The doctors had notified the family that her long battle with leukemia would soon be over. I entered her hospital room and moved slowly to the bed, noticing the monitors that showed her vital signs were constantly weakening. Even a young, inexperienced pastor knew it was only a matter of hours.

I had been so focused on the frail patient lying in the bed that I was startled to see her husband standing in the darkened shadows across the room. I knew the woman well but had little knowledge of her husband other than he was not a believer and had not attended church with his wife. I understood that I needed to offer words of comfort. I moved to his side and quoted several familiar biblical texts, assuring him that his wife would soon be in the presence of God.

His response was curt but honest: "Pastor Hemphill, you wouldn't find it so easy to quote those verses if it was your wife lying in that bed." I knew that his rebuke came from his grief but it hurt nonetheless. The pain of the sting must have shown on my face for it prompted an unexpected kindness. He laid a hand on my shoulder and replied, "Your presence here is enough." Sometimes words are not necessary. Walking along life's road during crisis and sharing joy and pain are sufficient.

By now you have discovered that this book is about a new approach to evangelism. It is a natural approach requiring sensitivity to the occasion and a strategic plan to build relationships that enable us to *splash* people with Living Water. While it is natural, it is at the same moment supernaturally empowered. It is not about sharing a presentation; it is about sharing Jesus who flows out of our life. Sharing life mandates that we love people and feel empathy for them; it requires a commitment of time; it means that we are willing to put the needs of others above our own; and it requires that we take the risk of vulnerability. To share with others about the One who is Life, we must be willing to share ourselves.

When Paul wrote to the Thessalonian community, he described his ministry among them in terms of a nursing mother who nurtures her own children. He then expresses the depth of his care: "Having so fond an affection for you, we were well-pleased to impart to you not only the Gospel of God but also our own lives, because you had become very dear to us" (1 Thessalonians 2:8). To be effective in reaching our colleagues, friends, and neighbors we must be willing to share our own lives with them.

Sharing Requires Love and Empathy

Empathy for others flows out of our commitment to love people as God loves them. We have already examined the mandate of love in an earlier section. We need to remind ourselves that Jesus loved us unconditionally, even when we were undeserving of His love: "For while we were still helpless, at the right time Christ died for the ungodly" (Romans 5:6). Thus, our love for our unsaved friend does not have to be deserved or merited.

In truth, it is our understanding of the power and the consequences of sin that compels us to share life with the people around us. We understand that man without the indwelling Holy Spirit is capable of all sorts of sinful attitudes and behavior. We should not be deterred from sharing life with people because they are rude or hateful or angry. Those behavioral issues should draw us to them all the more. We know the underlying cause of their rebellion is their sinful nature. Further, we know that we have the only solution to their underlying problem—it is Jesus we intend to share. Finally, we know if that solution for the sin problem is not accepted, the final consequence is eternal separation from God in hell, an unspeakable horror. Jesus suffered and died to deliver mankind from hell. His work on the cross defeated Satan and his power to hold man in bondage to sin. As Jesus' disciples we must be willing to suffer any affliction and do whatever it takes to share the good news of Jesus' power over sin and hell.

Before Jesus commissioned and sent His disciples to announce "The kingdom of heaven is at hand" (Matthew 10:7b), He shared with them His passion and His vision: "Seeing the people, He felt compassion for them, because they were distressed and dispirited like sheep without a shepherd" (Matthew 9:36). Jesus understood the condition of sheep without a shepherd. A sheep without a shepherd had no chance of survival. He would be mauled by a bear or lion or stolen and eaten by a thief. The words translated mildly as "weary and worn out" can be more literally translated as "torn and thrown down." The source of Jesus' relentless ministry activity is traced to His compassion for people who are blinded by sin and will be "torn and thrown down" by the adversary.

Jesus gives the disciples the good news followed by the bad news: "The harvest is plentiful, but the workers are few" (Matthew 9:37). We can have confidence in the awesome truth that the harvest of people is huge! The challenge is not the harvest, but the need for willing workers to gather God's crop of souls. Are we unwilling because we don't fully understand the consequences of sin? Do we lack compassion? If so, we must follow the directions of the Master: "Therefore beseech the Lord of the harvest to send out workers into His harvest" (9:38). We are not praying that God will send "someone else" but that He will send us. We are asking Him to help us see people through His eyes and minister in His name.

In 2 Corinthians 5:14, Paul states that Christ's love compels us so we would no longer live for ourselves but for the One who died for us. In this same context, Paul declares that we are ambassadors for Christ and, as such, we can be certain that God has given us the ministry of reconciliation. This understanding causes the believer to plead with those separated from God on Christ's behalf. Do you feel such compassion for the lost that you are willing to beg them to come to Christ?

The various encounters we have looked at concerning the ministry of Jesus flow out of His empathy and compassion. The widow whose only son had died would have been destitute without a male provider (Luke 7:11-15). The lame, the blind, and the diseased were outcasts. The woman caught in adultery would have been stoned to death. Zacchaeus was wealthy but friendless. Jesus saw behind the façade and shared Himself.

Sharing Life Requires the Willingness to Sacrifice

I have had the opportunity to visit the Holy Land on several occasions. I am continually impressed by the rugged and inhospitable topography. I am reminded that Jesus' ministry required physical, emotional, and spiritual stamina. It is possible that some of us avoid sharing life simply because we are unwilling to make the sacrifice necessary to be available to others. Or could it be that we are spiritually unfit? Sharing life demands a willingness to sacrifice and requires spiritual stamina. We will have to get our hands dirty with the filth that attaches itself to sin. Sharing life can be messy.

You may recall that Jesus ministered to the woman at the well while the disciples went to find food. When they returned and found Him talking to a woman they were amazed (John. 4:27). They then urged Jesus to eat but He responded that He had food they don't know about (32). The disciples wondered if someone else brought Him food. Listen to Jesus' response: "My food is to do the will of Him who sent Me and to accomplish His work" (34). Jesus was willing to sacrifice concerning His physical needs to meet the spiritual needs of the woman.

Don't miss the good news! The Father supplied all His needs. Jesus' kingdom-focused life mandated that He finish the Father's work—that means the Father was working to bring this Samaritan woman to Himself, and Jesus joined Him in that task. As a result, He was filled by the joy and satisfaction of obedience.

This story of the Samaritan woman is not finished. She returns to her hometown, telling her story about how she received Living Water: "From that city many of the Samaritans believed in Him because of the word of the woman who testified, 'He told me all the things that I have done.'" (4:39). Further we are told that the Samaritans asked Jesus to stay and He remained with them an additional two days (4:40). This must have been quite a sacrifice of precious time for One who had only three years of earthly ministry. The results make the sacrifice seem inconsequential. Many more Samaritans believed that Jesus really is the Savior of the world. The divine interruption yielded a spiritual harvest.

Recently, Paula and I had the privilege of visiting friends from a former church. One friend is a wonderful surgeon and works untold hours. When we asked why he didn't hire additional surgeons to provide some relief, he commented that he had been searching for other doctors to join his practice. The problem? The first question prospects asked was about the schedule. When told that they must be willing to do "whatever it takes" to meet the needs of the patients, they were suddenly uninterested in the job.

Are we willing to do "whatever it takes" to share Him? Jesus is worth sharing. I imagine that we would also agree that the eternal consequences for those dying without Him mandate that we share Him. If we know and serve the King, we have no other option. We must be willing to pay the price required to share Him until the whole world knows. When we remember what Jesus sacrificed to leave heaven and come to earth for the sole purpose of dying for our sins, we must agree that no price is too high for us.

Sharing Him Requires that We Put the Needs of Others Above Our Own

I grew up with a formula for life that was based on the acrostic "JOY." It stood for Jesus first; Others second, and You last. In our "me first" world, this sounds as dated as a rerun of *Father Knows Best*. Yet, this little acrostic clearly reflects the view of Scripture for the kingdom-focused person.

When Paul wrote to the church at Philippi, he asks several questions which assume a positive response: "Therefore if there is any encouragement in Christ, if there is any consolation of love, if there is any fellowship of the Spirit, if any affection and compassion…" (Philippians 2:1). Based on the assumed agreement to all these statements, Paul calls the members of the church at Philippi to "Do nothing from selfishness or empty conceit, but with humility of mind regard one another as more important than yourselves; do not merely look out for your own personal interests, but also for the interests of others" (2:3-4). To fortify this call to put the needs of others before our own, Paul calls believers to adopt the attitude of Christ Himself. Take a moment to meditate on the following text:

> Who, although He existed in the form of God, did not regard equality with God a thing to be grasped, but emptied Himself, taking the form of a bond-servant, and being made in the likeness of men. Being found in appearance as a man, He humbled Himself by becoming obedient to the point of death, even death on a cross. For this reason also, God highly exalted Him, and bestowed on Him the name which is above every name, so that at the name of Jesus EVERY KNEE WILL BOW, of those who are in heaven and on earth and under the earth, and that every tongue will confess that Jesus Christ is Lord, to the glory of God the Father (6-11).

When we remember the sacrifice Christ made for our redemption, we know that any sacrifice called for in sharing Him is small in comparison. If we manifested this attitude of putting the needs of others before our own needs, we could see "every tongue confess that Jesus Christ is Lord" in our generation. Don't forget that when you give, it is given to you, pressed down and running over. When we put others' needs before our own, we will find sacrifice a privilege and experience God's provision of a "food" that exceeds all our needs.

Sharing Him Requires a Willingness to be Vulnerable

Sharing is always a two-way street. Getting involved in the lives of others requires that we be willing to be vulnerable. When the woman with the issue of blood grabbed the cloak of Jesus, He knew that power had gone out of Him. Yes, ministry is costly. In our case, our attempts at showing love and sharing Him often reveal our own inadequacies and vulnerabilities. They unveil our fears. We are afraid that someone may reject our attempt to share Him. We are worried about our reputation. We are afraid that we may fail.

Someone we minister to may take advantage of us. I think you can take that as a guarantee. Remember that fallen man is prey to all the desires of the flesh without the power of the Spirit to restrain Him. So, don't be surprised when those you minister to choose to misuse or abuse you.

We sometimes gloss over the hard passages like Matthew 10. When Jesus sent His disciples out into the towns and villages as His representatives, He gave them fair warning. He told them to expect persecution, misunderstanding, betrayal, and hatred (16-23). This doesn't sound like the normal recruitment speech. The bottom line: "A disciple is not above his teacher, nor a slave above his master. It is enough for the disciple that he become like his teacher, and the slave like his master" (24-25a).

Take the time to read the passage in its entirety and you will find that it is filled with wonderful promises of God's sufficiency. The Spirit of our Father will speak through us (20), the Father will watch over us casting out all fear (26-31), and Christ will one day acknowledge us before the Father (32). You can never fail in God's eyes when you obediently join Him in splashing people with Living Water. The seed you sow when you share Him is good seed, and it will never return void. Trust God to give the results in His own time.

Here's another wonderful promise to consider when you take the *SPLASH* challenge—"He who has found his life will lose it, and he who has lost his life for My sake will find it" (39). You can find life worth living.

Technology gives this generation of believers new options for sharing Jesus with friends and colleagues. A pastor told us recently of a high school girl in his church who wanted to be honest with her friends about her relationship with God. She wrote the following on her *facebook* page:

"Moving on, I am a pretty devoted Christian and I never know how to tell people that without sounding cliché. When I was younger, I used to think it was my job to recruit everyone around me for Jesus, and even though I do play a role in my friends' salvation, I'm not so hung up on it anymore. If He's not for you, that's cool, but He is for me and I'm not going to tolerate Jesus bashing and whatnot. You might not believe the Bible has credibility, but you can't deny what God has done in my life. And if you are wondering, here's the time line of my 'spiritual journey,' before I knew Him, I was sad. Now I'm happy. Period!"

The evidence of this teenager's changed life gives credibility to her bold sharing. Her sharing also gives

SPLASH SHOW PEOPLE LOVE AND SHARE HIM

her accountability with her friends who watch her life for the transforming power of the Gospel.

Your Turn

Do you ask Jesus to show you opportunities to share? Read Colossians 4:2-4. What does being devoted to prayer have to do with open doors to share with others? Do you have difficulty thinking clearly when you talk about spiritual things? How can prayer help prepare you to share "in the way you ought to speak"? What do you think Paul means when he says your speech should be filled with "grace"? (Col. 4:6)

_____

_____

_____

_____

_____

What did you find most challenging about this section?

_____

_____

_____

_____

Do you see people with the eyes of Jesus? Who do you know who is like a sheep without a shepherd?

_____

_____

_____

_____

_____

What sacrifice have you made to share Him?

_____

_____

_____

_____

What further sacrifices do you believe may be required, and how does that make you feel?

_____

_____

_____

_____

SPLASH Show People Love And Share Him

Why is it so difficult to put the needs of others before our own needs?

_____

_____

_____

_____

_____

Reflections

Jesus said, "The harvest is abundant but the workers are few." Is this still true today? Why?

_____

_____

_____

_____

_____

Read Philippians 2:1-11 again. What did Paul mean when he instructed us to have the mind of Christ?

_____

_____

_____

_____

_____

List sacrifices that might be required to build a relationship with an unsaved friend or neighbor you identified in your *Splash Zone.*

_____

_____

_____

_____

_____

Recount a time recently when you sacrificed to show or share Christ with a friend and found that Christ was more than sufficient to supply your every need.

_____

_____

_____

_____

_____

Assignment

What sacrifice will you make this week to strengthen your relationship with someone in your *Splash Zone?* Share this with your Splash Effectiveness Partner and pray together for the Lord to give you opportunity and boldness. Be prepared to share the results next week.

HIM

Ken and I relocated to Tennessee and settled into a condominium in 2003. As we moved in, our neighbor Marge came tooling up in her bright green Volkswagen bug and introduced herself. Several weeks later I invited Marge to eat Sunday leftovers while Ken was out of town. For two hours Marge talked about her life and interests. A widow with three grown daughters, Marge attended First Baptist occasionally and enjoyed our pastor's sermons. She grew up in a liturgical tradition and raised her daughters in church in California. When I could get a word in edgewise I "splashed" the story of how God led us to Tennessee from Texas and how He provided this home in His plan. I shared Scripture and we laughed and enjoyed a pleasant evening getting to know each other.

Months later I baked cranberry orange bread and Ken and I delivered Christmas cards with the bread and his book *The Prayer of Jesus* to the neighbors in our cul de sac. Marge was visiting her daughter out west. When she returned home, I called to bring over her gift. She wasn't feeling well so I left the package on the bench by her door. The next morning my phone rang. Marge loved the book. She told me, "I have prayed the Lord's Prayer my whole life, but I did not know what it meant until I read Ken's book. Can I have three more copies for my daughters?"

Ken and I chose to pray for Marge daily. Because we traveled about 250 days a year with our work, we saw Marge sporadically. It was almost a year later before we had another opportunity to "splash" into her life.

In the fall Marge was diagnosed with cancer. She was hospitalized and came home right before Thanksgiving. I took a sweet potato casserole which her daughter said she might like. I knew Marge was seriously ill and did not have a church home in Tennessee. I offered her daughter Ken's help if the family needed a pastor in the coming days.

Monday Ken and I left for Florida where we intended to be until the next weekend. God had other plans! Our pastor in Tennessee was ill and needed Ken to preach. We flew home on Wednesday. On arriving home, we learned of Marge's death. We were stunned and saddened that we had not visited with her and shared the peace of Christ in a more verbal witness.

Ken was asked to officiate at Marge's funeral. As we met with the family to prepare for the service, we asked God to give us a clear understanding of Marge's spiritual life. The girls shared that in the last days of her life Marge often said she was "going home." She would become agitated and insist she needed a hat. In response to her demands, the girls would wet a washcloth and put it on her head. Instantly she became calm and rested peacefully. Finally, the daughters remembered their childhood trips to church when Marge always wore a hat. To go into God's presence and to go home, she needed a hat! How good God is to comfort His children with simple memories. At the end of her life, Marge splashed us with assurance of her relationship with God through Christ.

Leftovers and Christmas gifts became simple tools for showing Marge love and sharing Him. How can you open a door of hospitality to your neighbors and *SPLASH* them with Christ's love and share how He has moved in your life?

Mark recounts the healing of Simon's mother-in-law in the first chapter of his gospel, thus giving it great visibility. The healing is told with brevity as one would expect of this action-packed gospel. After word of the healing spread, people from the surrounding community begin to arrive at Simon's house in such large numbers that Mark declares, "And the whole city had gathered at the door" (1:33). As a result, Jesus continues to heal persons late into the evening.

The next morning, Jesus gets up before sunrise to go to a deserted place to pray. When the disciples discover that He is missing, they begin to search for Him. They come with an urgent message—"Everyone is looking for You" (1:37). His response to this announcement may surprise you; it certainly surprised His disciples: "Let us go somewhere else to the towns nearby, so that I may preach there also; for that is what I came for" (1:38).

What would you have done if you had been in His place, knowing you could meet all the physical needs of so many people? Meeting physical needs is important and gratifying, but we must not neglect doing the "best thing"—sharing Him. Jesus maintained His focus because He stayed in constant contact with His Father, and He kept man's spiritual condition in focus. If we do not *share* Him, we only meet the temporal needs of man. Think about it this way—we are not actually showing people love if we ignore their spiritual needs.

In Luke's gospel, after Jesus drives out a demon that caused a man to be mute, speculation arises among the Pharisees about His work of casting out demons. Jesus immediately points them to the power of God. He also seizes the moment to describe what would happen if an unclean spirit was cast out but nothing was put into the void left by the departure of the demon. The demon would return and find the house swept and put in order and bring seven other demons to inhabit the house. The sobering conclusion—"the last state of that man becomes worse than the first" (11:26b). When we meet people's physical or emotional needs and neglect their spiritual ones, we leave them in a condition worse than the one in which we found them. We have raised their hopes in this life, but have failed to tell them about the life to come, the very one they were created to enjoy for eternity.

If we are to be effective in sharing Him, we must remember:

- It is not just about being good and doing good
- It is not about the presentation of a set of propositions, but the sharing of a person
- It is not about religion but about a relationship with Him—Jesus!

Most secular people have rejected religion, not a relationship with God through Christ. We have good news. When we share our story in the power of the Holy Spirit, witnessing becomes as natural as splashing our friends with the exuberant overflow of the Living Water that comes from our inner being.

Learn From the Master

Think about the entire earthly ministry of Jesus, and you will find that His singular purpose was to introduce people to His Father as the source of all life. When the woman at the well wanted to know why a Jewish man was asking a favor of a Samaritan woman, Jesus' reply pointed her to the only source of Living Water: "If you knew the gift of God, and who it is who says to you, 'Give Me a drink,' you would have asked Him, and He would have given you living water" (John 4:10).

Likewise, when the Jews began persecuting Jesus for healing the man by the pool of Bethesda on the Sabbath, He tells them that He has simply joined in the work of His Father already in progress (John 5:19). Then He declares, "Truly, truly, I say to you, he who hears My word, and believes Him who sent Me, has eternal life, and does not come into judgment, but has passed out of death into life" (John 5:24). Once again, He points them to the Father who can give eternal life.

After they witnessed the feeding of the 5000, the crowd seeks Him out on the next day, looking for another hand-out. Jesus points them beyond the need for physical bread: ""Do not work for the food which perishes, but for the food which endures to eternal life, which the Son of Man will give to you, for on Him the Father, God, has set His seal" (John 6:27). When they ask Jesus for this bread, He replies, "I am the bread of life; he who comes to Me will not hunger, and he who believes in Me will never thirst" (John 6:35).

After rescuing the woman taken in adultery, He warns her not to sin anymore and then announces, "I am the Light of the world; he who follows Me will not walk in the darkness, but will have the Light of life" (John 8:12). The Pharisees try to avoid the obvious implications of His message by arguing that He has testified to Himself and, therefore, His testimony is not valid (8:14). His response—"You know neither Me nor My Father; if you knew Me, you would know My Father also" (8:19b).

When Jesus announces His impending departure, His disciples are a bit disconcerted. He promises that He is preparing a place for them and He will come again to enable them to come be with Him. Thomas protests that they don't know where He is going and, therefore, cannot know the way: "Jesus said to him, 'I am the way, and the truth, and the life; no one comes to the Father but through Me'" (John 14:6).

Jesus consistently used the meeting of physical needs as the bridge to revealing and meeting the deeper spiritual needs of man. We must learn from the Master and point people to Him. He is the only way to the Father.

The Command of the Master

One of the more dramatic healings of Jesus' earthly ministry involves a demon-possessed man. Most people avoided him. He wore no clothes and lived among the tombs, bound by chains and shackles. When Jesus casts the legion of demons out of him, they enter into a herd of pigs that then hurl themselves off a cliff into the lake and drown. The men who tended the pigs tell the townspeople what has happened, and they rush to the scene. The man who was healed is sitting at Jesus' feet, dressed and in his right mind.

When Jesus gets into the boat to leave, the healed man begs Jesus to allow him to follow Him. We are surprised when Jesus turns him away until we hear the explanation behind the refusal: "Return to your house and describe what great things God has done for you" (Luke 8:39a). An essential element of sharing Him is the recounting of your story. Never underestimate the power of your personal story.

My mentor, Mark Corts, developed an outreach strategy similar to Evangelism Explosion. A member on one of our ladies' teams missed visitation, and thus a relatively new Christian was recruited to go along as a silent prayer partner. This team visited the home of a professor of a local university who was an adamant and belligerent skeptic. At every turn of the conversation, he interjected his objections about the veracity of the Bible. These ladies were clearly outmatched. Suddenly and without warning, the "silent partner" challenged the professor by sharing her personal testimony about the radical transformation Jesus brought to her life. She sat back startled by her own boldness, expecting to be blasted for being so naïve. Unexpectedly, the professor slumped back into his chair and stated, "That's what bothers me about you Christians; I can't refute your story." Don't underestimate the power of your testimony told in the power of the Holy Spirit.

Lose Your Life to Gain It

When I was President of Southwestern Seminary, I was asked by several students if I ever found it difficult to witness to the unsaved. Much to their relief, I had to admit that I often found it challenging and would occasionally avoid people to escape my responsibility. My confession made them feel better, but it raised the question for all of us. Why are we so hesitant to share "good news?"

As we discussed our reluctance to share, we spoke about issues related to approaches that seemed too "canned." Witnessing should be natural. But the bottom line is that we "fear" man more than we fear God. We are afraid we may be rejected or even shunned because of our witness. Fear is real, and the adversary will use it to keep us silent. We must confront fear in the power of the Holy Spirit. Thus, prayer becomes an essential component of all our attempts to *Show People Love And Share Him*.

A text that might help keep a balanced perspective is Luke 9:23-27. This text is found in the context of Peter's confession that Jesus is God's Messiah. You may recall that this sublime confession was followed by the startling announcement that the Son of Man must face rejection, suffering, and death. These would lead to His glorious resurrection. While Luke doesn't mention it, Matthew tells us that Peter rebuked Jesus for the suggestion that He would suffer and die.

In this highly charged atmosphere, Jesus teaches His disciples that anyone who chooses to follow Him must deny himself, and take up his cross every day, and follow Him. Jim Elliot, a missionary who was killed by the Auca Indians, said it this way, "He is no fool who gives what he cannot keep to gain what he cannot lose." Jesus asks a probing question: "For what is a man profited if he gains the whole world, and loses or forfeits himself?" (Luke 9:25).

No doubt, you may be wondering what this has to do with the subject of witnessing. Listen to the next statement! "For whoever is ashamed of Me and My words, the Son of Man will be ashamed of him when He comes in His glory, and the glory of the Father and of the holy angels" (9:26). I don't want my pride or my fear to cause me to be ashamed of the Son of Man who died in my place. I certainly don't want Him to be ashamed of me.

Promises to Encourage You

Your witness has the power of the mustard seed and yeast. I know that this doesn't sound too impressive, but think through it. Jesus compared the kingdom of God to the power of the mustard seed and the penetrating power of yeast (Matt. 13:31-33). How amazing it is when a man plants a tiny mustard seed and it grows to a tree of such grandeur that the birds nest in its branches. A little yeast mixed into fifty pounds of flour leavens the entire mixture.

I stood on the balcony with some friends in Central Asia. We surveyed the buildings stretching out to the horizon and counted the many mosques by their towering minarets. Although we saw a large number of mosques, there were no visible churches in this predominantly Muslim country. Only a handful of believers have sensed God's call to show love and share Him in this area of the world. Thinking like the typical pastor, I asked how so few could ever reach so many. My friend replied, "All that is necessary to reach this country is to introduce the yeast of the Gospel and allow it to do its work."

You may think your small *splash* of Living Water will make no discernible difference in the vast ocean of unbelief, but if a little leaven can penetrate a vast quantity of flour and a little seed can produce a large tree, be assured that your witness will have vast kingdom impact. You may have the joy of sharing with the next Billy Graham. None of us will know this side of eternity the kingdom impact of the seed we sow.

Trust the power of God's Word. Do you believe God's Word is truth without any mixture of error? Then, listen to these promises:

• And that from childhood you have known the sacred writings which are able to give you the wisdom that leads to salvation through faith which is in Christ Jesus. All Scripture is inspired by God and profitable for teaching, for reproof, for correction, for training in righteousness (2 Timothy 3:15-16).

• For the word of God is living and active and sharper than any two-edged sword, and piercing as far as the division of soul and spirit, of both joints and marrow, and able to judge the thoughts and intentions of the heart (Hebrews 4:12).

- For I am not ashamed of the gospel, for it is the power of God for salvation to everyone who believes, to the Jew first and also to the Greek (Romans 1:16).

Did you notice what all these verses have in common? They tell us that the power is in Scripture, not in the eloquence of our presentation or in the impact of our illustrations. You don't need to have all the answers to the skeptic's questions; the Word has all the answers. Here's what Isaiah the prophet said about God's word: "So will My word be which goes forth from My mouth; It will not return to Me empty, without accomplishing what I desire, and without succeeding in the matter for which I sent it" (Isaiah 55:11). Just sow the seed and trust God to give the results.

Trust the power of the Spirit. I have frequently told young pastors that I think I am a pretty good pastor, but I know that I am a bad imitation for the Holy Spirit. You may not understand the point, but they do. Sometimes, we forget that it is the work of the Holy Spirit to bring conviction, and, thus, we try to manipulate persons to make spiritual decisions. You don't need to try to convince persons concerning their sinful condition or their need for a Savior. That is the work of the Holy Spirit. Here's a promise from the Master on which you can fully rely: "And He, when He comes, will convict the world concerning sin and righteousness and judgment; concerning sin, because they do not believe in Me" (John 16:8-9).

Rely on the Spirit to use others to SPLASH Living Water. I've got some great news for you. You are not alone in the work of sharing Him. There are countless thousands upon thousands of believers who daily attempt to share Christ. When you splash Living Water, you may be planting the seed. At other times, you may be watering seed that has been sown by someone else unknown to you. If you continue to *splash* Living Water, you will occasionally have the opportunity to reap the results of sowing and watering. It may take several *splashes* of Living Water before a person comes to the place where he is prepared to accept Christ as his personal Savior. You can trust the Spirit to continue to send persons to water and harvest every seed that is sown.

It has been my experience that few people actually pray to receive Christ on their first exposure to the Gospel. You may be privileged to be there for the harvest, but a parent, a sibling, or a childhood friend may have sown the original seed as they *splashed* a little Living Water. Just determine to do your part and trust the effectiveness of the seed, the power of the Word, the power of the Spirit, and the ministry of others.

Here's a simple formula for effectively sharing Him. Your story plus God's Word undergirded by the Holy Spirit equals a rich harvest.

Your Turn

As we think over our study together we need to keep in mind that *SPLASH* has both a spontaneous and a strategic component. Ask God to sensitize you to the daily opportunities to Show People Love And Share Him. When you have opportunity to see these people over an extended time period, ask Him to help you create a strategic plan for developing a relationship which meets needs and further enables you to share Him.

Let's brainstorm about a few action plans.

• Write out your testimony so that you can share it in 45 seconds or less. Make sure that it focuses on personal relationship and not religion. Avoid religious language that might not be understood.

• Print your testimony on a card or small piece of paper and include it in birthday cards, Christmas cards, and other greeting cards.

• Buy art and calligraphy that has a Christian theme and display it in your home. As you invite unsaved friends to your home, they will often ask about these items. Even if they don't, God can use them to *splash* your guests with Living Water.

• Get a supply of simple tracts that you can give to people you encounter every day. Better yet, write your own tract. You can get these printed relatively inexpensively.

- Mark your Bible with the plan of salvation. One example is what has been called the Roman Road. (See Appendix 1).

- Buy books that have ministered to you with the goal of giving them away. I have found that people may turn down or discard a tract, but they will not do so when offered a book. Paula and I have given *The Prayer of Jesus* and *He Is* to numerous friends. The *Kingdom Promise Series* I wrote which includes the titles *He Is*, *We Are*, *We Can*, and *But God*—were designed to be evangelistic gifts. Each of them has the plan of salvation in the back. Appendix 2 shows you how to use the *He Is* book as a witnessing tool.

- Take a witnessing class at your church. The more ways that you learn to share Him, the more comfortable and creative you will become in *splashing* your friends. If your church doesn't offer such a class, check out the website gotlife.com. The Action Gear offers a CD that will allow you to train yourself. This is the same presentation that occurs in the *Kingdom Promise Series*.

- Offer to pray for folks when they tell you about a need. Don't just promise to pray; do it right then when appropriate. Ask your waitress or waiter if there is any way you can pray for them as you prepare to ask your blessing.

- Get creative and let God show you His daily kingdom appointments for you.

Reflections

Why did Jesus find a place alone for prayer rather than returning to the needy crowd gathered at Simon's house?

_____

_____

_____

_____

_____

Look back at the "Promises to Encourage You." Which one did you find most challenging to act upon?

_____

_____

_____

_____

_____

Take the time to write your personal testimony so that you can share it in under one minute. Avoid terms that might be unclear to a person unfamiliar with the Bible. (See Appendix 3 for your testimony page).

_____

_____

_____

_____

_____

I have listed several ideas that might be effective in splashing people. In your small groups, share additional ideas for individually *splashing* people with Living Water.

_____

_____

_____

_____

_____

Get with your SEP and pray for one person in your splash zone who you plan to see this week.

Assignment

Congratulations on the completion of this study. It is my prayer that you have already discovered the effectiveness of the *SPLASH* strategy. I would ask that you sign the covenant card indicating your desire to share Christ with one person in your Splash Zone with the goal of leading them to faith in Christ this year. I am praying that you will find that *SPLASH* becomes a lifestyle of participating in kingdom advance. Your family can share ideas and build relationships together for the sake of the King and the advance of His kingdom. I would further suggest that you continue to meet with your SEP for prayer, sharing of ideas, and accountability. Happy *SPLASHing*!

APPENDIX 1

Roman Road

Man is a sinner.
"As it is written, 'THERE IS NONE RIGHTEOUS, NOT EVEN ONE;'" (Romans 3:10)

"For all have sinned and fall short of the glory of God." (Romans 3:23)

The penalty for sin is death.
"Therefore, just as through one man sin entered into the world, and death through sin, and so death spread to all men, because all sinned—" (Romans 5:12)

"For the wages of sin is death, but the free gift of God is eternal life in Christ Jesus our Lord." (Romans 6:23)

Christ came and paid the penalty for sin.
"But God demonstrates His own love toward us, in that while we were yet sinners, Christ died for us." (Romans 5:8)

It is by believing in Christ that we experience His forgiveness.
"That if you confess with your mouth Jesus as Lord, and believe in your heart that God raised Him from the dead, you will be saved; for with the heart a person

SPLASH APPENDIX 1

believes, resulting in righteousness, and with the mouth he confesses, resulting in salvation." (Romans 10:9-10)

"For 'WHOEVER WILL CALL ON THE NAME OF THE LORD WILL BE SAVED.'" (Romans 10:13)

How to use the Roman Road:
One way to use this method of sharing the Gospel is to mark a New Testament. In the front or the back of the Bible, write: Man is a sinner. Turn to Romans 3:10.

On the page that you find Romans 3:10, write: Turn to Romans 3:23.

Continue in this method until you have a road map to guide you through this group of Scripture.

Another idea is to keep a copy of these verses on a card in your Bible to use as a guide.

APPENDIX 2

How to use the *He Is* book
as a witnessing tool

The following presentation is based on several simple questions and a personal testimony which focuses on relationship and not religion. It is powerful because it focuses throughout on the person of Jesus. He has promised that when He is lifted up, He will draw men to Himself.

Begin with this series of non-threatening questions:

1. Have you had the opportunity to begin reading the little book I gave you?

This is an ice-breaker question and you can continue the presentation whether they have read the book or not.

2. May I ask you a question? In your opinion, who is Jesus?

Opinion questions are generally non-threatening. You listen to their answer for a clue to their understanding of the person of Jesus. You can also affirm them for their answer. If it is completely off base you can simply say, "Well I am glad you have been thinking about Jesus."

105

3. May I ask who Jesus is to you?

The answer to this question will tell you whether they understand what it means to have a personal relationship with Christ. It is again non-threatening. Many non-Christians will respond that they do not understand the question. That response is a natural lead in to the next question.

4. May I tell you who Jesus is to me?

You have noticed that we are asking for and earning the right to share. At this point you simply share your personal testimony with an emphasis on relationship and not religion. It should be no more than one minute in length.

Here is a shortened sample of mine: I grew up in a Christian home. In fact, my dad was a Baptist preacher. For several years I thought that I was a Christian because I went to church and tried to be a good person. But I realized that I had sinned and that no amount of good works could make up for my sins. I began to understand the truth that Jesus had already paid for my sins and I invited Him into my life to be my personal savior. I now understand that what I needed was a relationship with God through His Son and not a religious experience.

5. Do you have the little book we gave you? I want to show you something I think you will find exciting.

You open the book to the back where you will find a

presentation of the Gospel based on the LIFE acrostic. I suggest you simply read the short plan of salvation. You can introduce it by saying something like this, "In the back of your book is a simple outline of some really good news. It will help you to understand how you can have a personal relationship with God." After you read the LIFE presentation, ask one final question.

I sometimes lead into the next question by saying— "When I discovered that I could have a personal relationship with God, have my sins forgiven, and be assured of heaven when I die, I thought that is too good an offer to refuse."

6. Can you think of any reason that you wouldn't like to establish a personal relationship with God right now?

You can then lead them in a simple sinner's prayer which is included in the book. You will also notice that there is a place for them to sign and date the book as a means of public confession. You could also indicate your willingness to witness their signature by signing below their signature.

If you are looking for a good simple follow-up tool to put in the hands of a new believer, look at the *We Are* volume in this series of Kingdom Promise books. It covers many of the things you want a new Christian to understand.

SPLASH APPENDIX 2

The two other titles, *We Can* and *But God* can also be used as evangelistic tools. They are particularly good little gifts to give to someone who is going through a challenging time. Both books have the plan of salvation in the back.

APPENDIX 3

How to write your testimony

For a biblical example, read Paul's testimony recorded in Acts 26.

Tell about your past before you became a Christian.

Tell how you came to know about Jesus and the change that He made in your life.

Explain your own personal experience in having a relationship with God through Christ.

Next to letting people see the change God has made in you, telling your own story is still the most powerful tool you have for sharing the Good News about Jesus. People might be able to counter your logical arguments for God, but nobody can tell you that your experience with God isn't real.

APPENDIX 4

SPLASH ZONE

Family Zone

The Family Zone consists of your immediate family—spouse, children and those living in your household—and also your extended family—grandparents, aunts, uncles, cousins, etc.

Existing Friendships Zone

The Existing Friendships Zone consists of those special people who are already in your life. Don't overlook the need for Christ among those you already know.

Neighborhood Zone

The Neighborhood Zone is filled with people who are near you physically. They can be people who live on your street or in your apartment building. These are people you have an opportunity to get to know because your paths cross regularly.

Workplace Zone

The Workplace Zone encompasses those you interact with in the course of the work-day. Think about ways you can SPLASH this group too.

APPENDIX 4 **SPLASH**

Affinity Zone

People in your Affinity Zone are those with whom you share a common interest. Think about those you encounter on the golf course, in the gym, in your civic organization, at a play group or at a club meeting.

Serendipity Zone

The Serendipity Zone consists of those you meet in a random situation. Maybe it is someone you may never see again. Think of people you meet on an airplane or while traveling, someone you encounter on the street or anyone that the Lord places in your path.

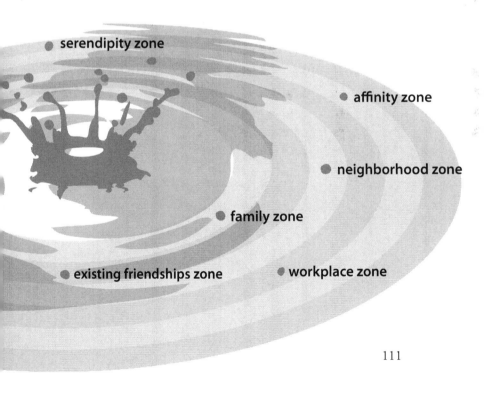

111

APPENDIX 5

SPLASH ZONE CARDS

Copy these cards on heavy paper and keep them as a reference and a reminder. Identify at least one person in each zone and write their name on the card.

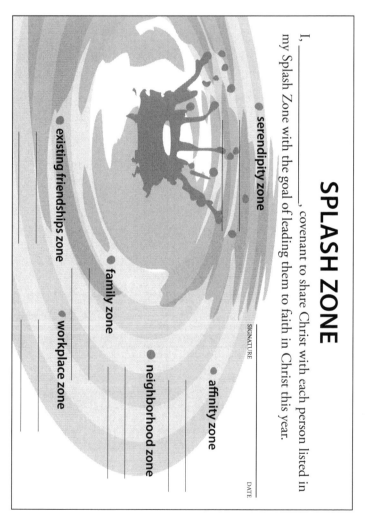

These cards will help you to keep track of people and *SPLASH* encounters as you develop your strategy to Show People Love And Share Him.

SHOW • PEOPLE • LOVE

Name of Person: _____

_____

Address/Phone: _____

_____

_____

_____

Birthday/Anniversary: _____

_____

Hobbies/Interests: _____

_____

Additional Information: _____

_____

AND • SHARE • HIM

Record SPLASH encounters here:

Date:_____

Details:_____

_____

_____

Date:_____

Details:_____

_____

_____

Date:_____

Details:_____

_____

_____

These cards are available for download on this website: www.splashinfo.com.

Made in the USA
Middletown, DE
03 March 2016